D1285009

THE GETTYSBURG ADDRESS
XIX NOVEMBER · MDCCCLXIII

☆

FOURSCORE & SEVEN YEARS AGO OUR FATHERS BROUGHT FORTH ON THIS CONTINENT A NEW NATION · CONCEIVED IN LIBERTY · AND DEDICATED TO THE PROPOSITION THAT ALL MEN ARE CREATED EQUAL·

NOW WE ARE ENGAGED IN A GREAT CIVIL WAR · TESTING WHETHER THAT NATION · OR ANY NATION SO CONCEIVED AND SO DEDICATED · CAN LONG ENDURE · WE ARE MET ON A GREAT BATTLE-FIELD OF THAT WAR · WE HAVE COME TO DEDICATE A PORTION OF THAT FIELD AS A FINAL RESTING PLĀCE FOR THOSE WHO HERE GAVE THEIR LIVES THAT THAT NATION MIGHT LIVE · IT IS ALTOGETHER FITTING & PROPER THAT WE SHOULD DO THIS·

BUT · IN LARGER SENSE · WE CANNOT DEDICATE — WE CANNOT CONSECRATE — WE CANNOT HALLOW — THIS GROUND· THE BRAVE MEN · LIVING AND DEAD · WHO STRUGGLED HERE HAVE CONSECRATED IT FAR ABOVE OUR POOR POWER TO ADD OR DETRACT · THE WORLD WILL LITTLE NOTE NOR LONG REMEMBER WHAT WE SAY HERE · BUT IT CAN NEVER FORGET WHAT THEY DID HERE · IT IS FOR US · THE LIVING · RATHER· TO BE DEDICATED HERE TO THE UNFINISHED WORK WHICH THEY WHO FOUGHT HERE HAVE THUS FAR SO NOBLY ADVANCED · IT IS RATHER FOR US TO BE HERE DEDICATED TO THE GREAT TASK REMAINING BEFORE US — THAT FROM THESE HONORED DEAD WE TAKE INCREASED DEVOTION TO THAT CAUSE FOR WHICH THEY GAVE THE LAST FULL MEASURE OF DEVOTION · THAT WE HERE HIGHLY RESOLVE THAT THESE DEAD SHALL NOT HAVE DIED IN VAIN · THAT THIS NATION · UNDER GOD · SHALL HAVE A NEW BIRTH OF FREEDOM · AND THAT GOVERNMENT OF THE PEOPLE · BY THE PEOPLE · FOR THE PEOPLE · SHALL NOT PERISH FROM THE EARTH ·

· ABRAHAM LINCOLN ·

THE BATTLE OF GETTYSBURG

The Country
The Contestants
The Results

by

DR. WILLIAM CLAYTON STORRICK, Litt D
Retired Superintendent of Guides:
Gettysburg National Park Commission

First Edition, 1931	Sixteenth Printing, 1956
Second Printing, 1935	Seventeenth Printing, 1957
Third Printing, 1938	Eighteenth Printing, 1959
Fourth Printing, 1944	Nineteenth Printing, 1959
Fifth Printing, 1945	Twentieth Printing, 1961
Sixth Printing, 1946	Twenty-first Printing, 1962
Seventh Printing, 1946	Twenty-second Printing, 1965
Eighth Printing, 1947	Twenty-third Printing, 1966
Ninth Printing, 1949	Twenty-fourth Printing, 1969
Tenth Printing, 1949	Twenty-fifth Printing, 1971
Eleventh Printing, 1951	Twenty-sixth Printing, 1972
Twelfth Printing, 1951	Twenty-seventh Printing, 1974
Thirteenth Printing, 1953	Twenty-eighth Printing, 1975
Fourteenth Printing, 1954	Second Edition, 1980
Fifteenth Printing, 1955	Second Printing, 1980

50th Anniversary Edition, 1981

Copyright © 1980, 1981, by Greenwood-Horne Publishing Co.
All rights reserved. This work may not be reproduced in any manner
without express permission of the publisher.

Printed in the United States of America

GREENWOOD-HORNE PUBLISHING CO.
P.O. Box 659
Barnegat, NJ 08005

DEDICATION

This second edition is dedicated to the memory of Miss Nina Storrick, eldest child of the author, who died peacefully in Gettysburg on May 10, 1980, and to Daniel, great-great-grandson of the author, who on June 5, 1980, turned three.

FOREWORD

NO ONE is better fitted to describe the Battle of Gettysburg and the National Park established on its site than Mr. William C. Storrick. Born a short distance from the field, he was seven years old at the time of the battle. He remembers the flight from home as the army drew near; he remembers also the return to a house which had been occupied by troops. Still more distinctly he recalls going to Gettysburg on November 19, standing with his hand clasped in his father's, watching a doorway from which the President of the United States was shortly to appear. He shook hands with Lincoln, was awed by his great height, and listened eagerly to his plain and simple address.

For more than twenty years Mr. Storrick was connected with the Battlefield Commission, first in charge of the farms, then of the guide service as well. The history of the campaign which forms a part of this volume was prepared at the request of the War Department.

There is no corner of the field which Mr. Storrick does not know; there is no detail of its history which he has not studied; there is no disputed question of which he cannot give both sides. His clear and uncontroversial account of the battle is but an outline of his store of information upon which he plans to draw more largely in a volume of greater scope.

ELSIE SINGMASTER LEWARS.

CONTENTS

THE BATTLE OF GETTYSBURG

IT IS difficult to present a great battle with sufficient detail to please both the student of tactics and the average reader. If the visitor is not satisfied with the brief outline here presented, he is recommended to read further in the books listed, and especially to employ a guide, without whose trained and supervised services the best manual is inadequate. The reader in search of romance is recommended to the successive Incidents of the Battle as herein presented.

According to official records, the Gettysburg campaign of 1863 began on June 3rd and ended on August 1st. No effort will be made to describe the movements, counter-movements, and fifty minor engagements that occurred before the armies crossed the Mason and Dixon's line and finally concentrated at Gettysburg, where they engaged in battle on July 1st, 2nd, and 3rd. It is necessary, however, that the visitor should understand the approach to the field.

LOCATION OF THE ARMIES.

On June 3rd the Union Army, called the Army of the Potomac, lay at Falmouth, Va., on the north side of the Rappahannock River, Major-General Joseph Hooker in command.

The Confederate Army, called the Army of Northern Virginia, occupied the south bank, with headquarters at Fredericksburg, General Robert E. Lee in command.

Both armies were resting after the major engagement at Chancellorsville, in which the Confederates were victorious.

The Army of the Potomac was made up of seven infantry and one cavalry corps. It numbered at the time of the battle approximately 84,000.

The Army of Northern Virginia was made up of three infantry corps and one division of cavalry. It numbered at the time of the battle about 75,000.

Following the text is a roster of officers, which should be consulted, both for an understanding of the battle and because of the obligation to honor brave men.

GENERAL LEE'S PLAN.

During the month of May, General Lee visited Richmond to discuss with the Confederate government various plans involving political and military considerations. Up to this time, the South had won the major victories, but her resources, both in men and sinews of war, were diminishing, and a prolonged conflict would be disastrous. It was decided that the army should invade the North via the Shenandoah and Cumberland valleys, with Harrisburg as an objective. This route not only afforded a continuous highway but put the army in a position to threaten Baltimore, Philadelphia, and Washington from the north. The Blue Ridge Mountains to the east would screen the advance, and the rich agricultural section would furnish supplies of food and forage.

The time was propitious. General Lee's army was in the prime of condition. The North was discouraged by losses, distrustful of Lincoln, weary of war. The South believed that one great victory would assure her the friendliness of the leading powers of Europe. Her independence once acknowledged, she could import the materials of war and the necessities of life which she lacked. It was thought certain that at the prospect of invasion the North would withdraw troops from the siege of Vicksburg then being conducted by General Grant. With high hopes the march was begun.

LEE'S FIRST MOVEMENT.

On June 3rd Lee put his army in motion northward, with Ewell's Corps, preceded by Jenkins' and Imboden's Cavalry, in the advance, followed by Longstreet and lastly by Hill. Longstreet moved on the east side of the Blue Ridge in order to lead Hooker to believe that Washington would be threatened. On reaching Snicker's Gap, he crossed the Ridge into the Shenandoah Valley and followed Hill, who was now in advance. The great army was strung out from Fredericksburg, Va., on the south to Martinsburg, W. Va., on the north, with the cavalry division under Stuart guarding the gaps along the Blue Ridge.

[6]

Since 1863 the population of Gettysburg has increased from 2,000 to 5,500

After driving out Union forces stationed at Winchester under Milroy, Lee's Army crossed the Potomac at Williamsport and Shepherdstown on June 23rd, 24th, and 25th, and advanced northward, unopposed, through the Cumberland Valley, toward Harrisburg.

HOOKER'S PLAN.

On June 10th, Hooker proposed to President Lincoln that he cross the Rappahannock and attack Hill, who still remained, and then move south, threatening Richmond. He thought this might divert Lee from his invasion of the North. In reply Lincoln said:

"I think Lee's Army and not Richmond is your sure objective point."

THE APPOINTMENT OF MEADE.

Thereupon Hooker started in pursuit of Lee on June 13th, moving east of the Blue Ridge on a line parallel with Lee on the west, with the cavalry guarding his left. He thus protected Baltimore and Washington. He crossed the Potomac at Edward's Ferry on the 25th and 26th and reached Frederick on the 27th, where he halted. Believing himself handicapped by orders from General Halleck, Chief in Command at Washington, who refused the use of the Union forces at Harper's Ferry, he asked to be relieved of the command of the Army of the Potomac. The request was granted, and, on June 28th, Major-General George G. Meade, in command of the 5th Corps, was appointed his successor, Sykes taking command of General Meade's Corps.

ADVANCE OF LEE.

Lee's Army had been steadily moving northward in the Cumberland Valley. Ewell, in the advance, detached Early's Division on reaching Chambersburg, directing him to move through Gettysburg on June 26th and thence to York and Wrightsville, there to cross the Susquehanna to Columbia and move up to Harrisburg to meet the divisions of Rodes and Johnson. Rodes reached Carlisle on June 28th, accompanied by Ewell; Johnson was at Greenvillage, between Chambersburg and Carlisle. Hill moved from Chambersburg to Cashtown, and Longstreet was in the rear at Chambersburg. Lee's headquarters were in Messersmith's Woods near Chambersburg.

In his advance into Gettysburg, Early was opposed by the 26th Emergency Regiment of Pennsylvania Volunteers, Company A, consisting of students of Pennsylvania (now Gettysburg) College, citizens of the town, and some volunteers from Harrisburg. After skirmishing on the Chambersburg Pike about 3 miles from the town, this regiment was obliged to retreat, finally reaching Harrisburg. About 175 were captured, but were afterward paroled.

GENERAL REYNOLDS' POSITION SHORTLY BEFORE HIS DEATH.—Near General Buford's statue, pointing toward the spectator, is the first gun fired by the Union forces

On the same day, George Sandoe, a Union scout, was shot by one of Early's pickets on the Baltimore Pike. He was the first Union soldier killed in the vicinity of Gettysburg prior to the battle.

On account of the absence of his cavalry under Stuart, who had been left with five brigades to guard the rear and hold the gaps of the Blue Ridge, Lee did not know until June 28th that the Union Army had crossed the Potomac and was threatening his line of communication with the South. Learning this, he ordered a concentration of his forces at Cashtown.

MEADE'S MOVEMENT.

On assuming command, General Meade moved his army northward from the vicinity of Frederick and established a tentative line along Pipe Creek, between Manchester on his right and Emmitsburg on his left, with headquarters near Taneytown.

STUART'S MOVEMENT.

After the Union Army crossed the Potomac, Stuart left the line of the Blue Ridge with three brigades of cavalry and made a raid around the Union Army, crossing the Potomac at Seneca Creek and moving thence to Hanover, where he engaged Kilpatrick's Division of Union cavalry on June 30th. Passing through Jefferson, Dover, and Dillsburg to Carlisle, he reached Carlisle on the afternoon of July 1st, getting into communication with Lee, after an interval of a week.

SITUATION OF CONFEDERATE FORCES ON JUNE 30TH.

On June 30th, Pender's Division, Hill's Corps, moved from Fayetteville to Cashtown; Anderson's Division to Fayetteville; Rodes' Division, Ewell's Corps, from Carlisle via Petersburg to Heidlersburg. Early's Division advanced from York through Weiglestown and East Berlin, and encamped 3 miles from Heidlersburg. Johnson's Division marched from Greenvillage to Scotland. Hood's and McLaws' Divisions, Longstreet's Corps, moved from Chambersburg to Fayetteville; Pickett's Division remained at Chambersburg. Lee's headquarters were at Greenwood.

SITUATION OF UNION FORCES ON JUNE 30TH.

On June 30th the 11th Corps was at Emmitsburg, the 1st at Marsh Creek, the 3rd at Bridgeport, the 5th at Union Mills, the

6th at Manchester, the 12th at Littlestown, the 2nd at Taneytown. Two brigades of Buford's Cavalry Division were at Gettysburg; Gregg's Cavalry Division was at Manchester; Kilpatrick's at Hanover. Meade's headquarters were at Taneytown.

THE PENNSYLVANIA MONUMENT, with bronze figures of distinguished officers and a roster of all Pennsylvanians in battle.

THE APPROACH.

Neither commander yet foresaw Gettysburg as a field of battle. Each had expected to take a strong position and force his adversary to attack. But in the hot summer weather fate was moving the mighty hosts closer and closer. The sky was cloudless, and the summer moon was at its brightest. The wheat was ripe, and the armies marched between partly reaped fields.

On the 30th, Hill, in the front at Cashtown, sent Pettigrew's Brigade to Gettysburg for supplies, shoes especially being badly needed. In the meantime, Meade ordered Buford, with two brigades of cavalry at Emmitsburg, to make a reconnaissance to Gettysburg. Buford reported:

"*I entered this place today at 11 A.M. Found everybody in a terrible state of excitement on account of the enemy's advance.*"

On reaching Seminary Ridge, Pettigrew saw the approach of Buford. Not wishing to bring on an engagement, he withdrew to the vicinity of Cashtown.

Buford moved through the town and bivouacked for the night west of the Seminary, along McPherson Ridge. He assigned to Gamble's Brigade the task of watching the Fairfield and Cashtown roads and to Devin the Mummasburg, Middletown (now Biglerville), and Harrisburg roads. Early on the morning of the 1st, he picketed all the roads leading north and northeast.

THE FIRST DAY

INFORMED by Pettigrew that Union forces had reached Gettysburg, and anxious to know their strength, Hill sent Heth's and Pender's Divisions with Pegram's battalion of artillery forward on a reconnaissance in force. This movement, made at 5.30 A.M. on July 1, precipitated the battle.

The advance was soon interrupted by Buford's skirmishers. On reaching Herr Ridge, which crosses the Cashtown Road at right angles, Hill deployed his line of battle—Heth on both sides of the road with Pender in reserve. Pegram posted his artillery on Herr Ridge, and at 8 o'clock fired his first shot. Buford's artillery, under Calef, posted on the opposite ridge, fired in reply. The battle was on, and the gravity of the situation was clear to Buford, who at 10.10 A.M. sent this message to Meade:

"The enemy's force are advancing on me at this point and driving my pickets and skirmishers very rapidly. There is a large force at Heidlersburg that is driving my pickets at that point from that direction. I am sure that the whole of A. P. Hill's force is advancing."

ARRIVAL OF REYNOLDS.

Union reinforcements were at hand. General Reynolds, in advance of the 1st Corps, arrived from Marsh Creek, via the Emmitsburg Road. After a short conference with Buford at the Seminary buildings, he sent an orderly urging Wadsworth, whose division was advancing across the fields, to hasten. On its arrival, Reynolds posted Cutler to the right, across the railroad cut which lies parallel to the Chambersburg Pike, and Meredith on the left. (Reynolds Avenue now marks this line.)

DEATH OF REYNOLDS.

After posting Hall's battery in place of Calef's, Reynolds rode to the McPherson Woods, and while directing the advance of Meredith at 10.15 A.M. was instantly killed by a Confederate sharpshooter. Doubleday consequently assumed command of the 1st Corps, and Rowley succeeded Doubleday in command of the Division. Compelled to fall back into the grove, Buford moved his cavalry to the left near the Fairfield Road, and Meredith advanced into the woods, drove Hill's right across Willoughby Run, and captured General Archer and part of his men.

On the Union right, Cutler was attacked in flank by Davis's Brigade, of the left of Hill's line, and was compelled to withdraw. Davis advanced into the railroad cut where part of his force was captured. He then withdrew to his original line.

GETTYSBURG SEMINARY DOORWAY.—The Lutheran Theological Seminary was used as an observation point and hospital. The portico was erected in 1913 to commemorate the fiftieth anniversary of the battle.

A MORNING LULL.

At 11 A.M. there was a lull. Doubleday withdrew his forces from across Willoughby Run and established a new line through the McPherson Woods from north to south. Robinson's Division reached the field and was held in reserve at the Seminary buildings. Rowley's Division (formerly Doubleday's) arrived a little later; Stone's Brigade of this Division was deployed in the front line on what is now Stone Avenue, and Biddle's Brigade was placed on the left of Meredith, along what is now South Reynolds Avenue. In the afternoon, Robinson's Division was moved to the right, prolonging the Union line to the Mummasburg Road in order to meet the advance of Rodes' Division, coming forward via the Carlisle Road. Devin's cavalry was moved from Buford's right to the vicinity of the York Pike and the Hanover Road.

In this preliminary action of the forenoon the advantage was in favor of the Union forces. The Confederate General Heth reported:

"The enemy had now been felt, and found in heavy force in and around Gettysburg. The division was now formed in line of battle on the right of the road; Archer's brigade on the right, Pettigrew's in the center, and Brockenbrough's on the left. Davis's brigade was kept on the left of the road that it might collect its stragglers, and from its shattered condition it was not deemed advisable to bring it again into action that day."

The Union General Buford reported:

"On July 1, between 8 and 9 A.M. reports came in from the 1st Brigade (Colonel Gamble's) that the enemy was coming down from toward Cashtown in force. Colonel Gamble made an admirable line of battle, and moved off proudly to meet him. The two lines soon became hotly engaged, we having the advantage of position, he of numbers. The 1st Brigade held its own for more than two hours, and had to be literally dragged back a few hundred yards to a more secure and sheltered position."

ARRIVAL OF RODES AND EARLY.

On learning at Middletown (now Biglerville) that Hill was engaged with the Union forces at Gettysburg, Rodes marched thither directly via the Carlisle Road. Early approached via the Harrisburg or Heidlersburg Road. The advance of both was quickened by the sound of cannonading. Arriving a little past noon, Rodes deployed his Division of five brigades on both sides of Oak Ridge, his right on the left of Heth's Division and his left with Early's right, extending across the plain north of the town. Carter's artillery was posted on Oak Hill.

THE OPPOSING LINES.

Robinson's Division of the 1st Union Corps was moved from its position in reserve at the Seminary buildings to the right of Cutler, to oppose Rodes's Confederate line.

Hill prolonged his right by bringing up Pender's Division that had been held in reserve. The artillery of McIntosh's battalion was brought into action in support. These guns, with Carter's and Pegram's, together numbering 60, and 11 brigades of infantry now opposed the 1st Union Corps of 36 guns and 6 brigades.

ARRIVAL OF HOWARD.

General Howard, in command of the 11th Union Corps, reached Gettysburg from Emmitsburg between 10 and 11 A.M., in advance of his Corps, and took command of the Union forces. Schurz succeeded Howard in command of the Corps, and Doubleday resumed command of his Division.

On reaching Gettysburg, Howard went to the top of the Fahnestock building at the corner of Baltimore and Middle streets to observe the lines of battle. He reported:

"I had studied the position a few moments, when a report reached me that General Reynolds was wounded. At first I hoped his wound might be slight

and that he would continue to command, but in a short time I was undeceived. His aid-de-camp, Major William Riddle, brought the sad tidings of his death. This was about 11.30 A.M. Prior to this the General had sent me orders to move up at a double quick, for he was severely engaged. On hearing of the death of Reynolds, I assumed command of the left wing, instructing General Schurz to take command of the 11th Corps. After an examination of the general features of the country, I came to the conclusion that the only tenable position for my limited force was the ridge to the southeast of Gettysburg (now well known as Cemetery Ridge). I at once established my headquarters near the cemetery, and on the highest point north of the Baltimore Pike."

HOWARD'S POSITION.

On the arrival of the 11th Corps, Howard ordered Schurz to move the 3rd and 1st Divisions to positions north of the town, while the 2nd Division was held on Cemetery Hill in reserve. On account of the prior arrival of the Confederates under Rodes, who covered the plain north of the town, Schurz was unable to connect with the right of the Union line on Oak Hill, and a gap remained between the two lines. The position of the 11th Corps coincides with what is now Howard Avenue.

THE CONFEDERATE GENERAL EARLY'S POSITION.

Shortly after the 11th Corps moved to the front, Early's Division of Ewell's Corps arrived from Heidlersburg and went into line to the right of Howard, connecting with Rodes's left across the plain. Early posted his artillery, Jones's battalion, in position to enfilade the right of Howard, while Carter's batteries on Oak Hill enfiladed the left. The Confederate forces largely exceeded the Union forces, the former being about 28,000 and the latter about 18,000. The whole Confederate line advanced and attacked the Union forces in front and on both flanks. On Oak Hill part of Rodes' forces, O'Neal's and Iverson's brigades, were repulsed, a large part of the latter being captured.

THE UNION RETREAT.

After a strenuous resistance the whole Union line was compelled to withdraw to Cemetery Hill. The 11th Corps retreated through the center of town where many were captured. The 1st Corps fell back through the western part of the town. By 4.30 P.M. all the territory held by the Union forces was occupied by the Confederates.

ARRIVAL OF LEE.

General Lee reached the field from Cashtown about 3 P.M., witnessed the retreat of the Union forces, and established his head-quarters in tents in an apple orchard back of the Seminary. He ordered Ewell to follow up the repulse if he thought it practicable. In this connection Ewell reported:

"The enemy had fallen back to a commanding position known as Cemetery Hill, south of Gettysburg, and quickly showed a formidable front there. On entering the town, I received a message from the Commanding General to attack this hill, if I could do so to advantage. I could not bring artillery to bear on it, and all the troops with me were jaded by twelve hours' marching and fighting, and I was notified that General Johnson's division (the only one of my corps that had not been engaged) was close to town. Cemetery Hill was not assailable from the town. . . . Before Johnson could be placed in position the night was far advanced."

General Hill reported:

"Under the impression that the enemy was entirely routed, my own two divisions exhausted by some six hours' hard fighting, prudence led me to be content with what had been gained."

JOHN BURNS, Gettysburg constable and Mexican War veteran, shouldered his musket and went out to meet the Confederates.

The failure of Ewell to follow up the repulse and capture Cemetery Hill and Culp's Hill, defended by a weak line of the Union forces, enabled the Union commanders to establish during the night a line of defence that was secure against attack. By many military critics, this is generally considered Lee's lost opportunity.

FORMATION OF UNION LINE.

The retreating Union soldiers were met at East Cemetery Hill by Generals Hancock and Howard, who directed them to positions, the 1st Corps on Cemetery Ridge and Culp's Hill, and the 11th on East Cemetery Hill. The 12th Corps arrived on the Baltimore Pike, and soon after Sickles' 3rd Corps came up from Emmitsburg.

Hancock had been instructed by Meade to take command and report if he thought the ground a suitable place to continue the battle. A battle-line was at once established on Cemetery Ridge. Geary's Division of the 12th Corps was ordered to the extreme left to occupy Little Round Top. Hancock sent word to General Meade that the position was strong, but that it might be easily turned. He then turned over the command to Slocum, his senior, and returned to Taneytown to report in person. Meade had already ordered a rapid concentration of all his forces at Gettysburg.

GENERAL LEE'S REPORT.

For the day, the Confederate commander reported:

"The leading division of Hill met the enemy in advance of Gettysburg on the morning of July 1. Driving back these troops to within a short distance of the town, he there encountered a larger force, with which two of his divisions became engaged. Ewell coming up with two of his divisions by the Heidlersburg road, joined in the engagement. The enemy was driven through Gettysburg with heavy loss, including about 5,000 prisoners and several pieces of artillery. He retired to a high range of hills south and east of the town. The attack was not pressed that afternoon, the enemy's force being unknown, and it being considered advisable to await the arrival of the rest of our troops. Orders were sent back to hasten their march, and, in the meantime, every effort was made to ascertain the numbers and position of the enemy, and find the most favorable point of attack. It had not been intended to fight a general battle at such a dis-

BARLOW'S KNOLL.—The extreme right of the Union line on the first day

*tance from our base, unless attacked by the enemy, but, finding ourselves
unexpectedly confronted by the Federal Army, it became a matter of difficulty
to withdraw through the mountains with our large trains. . . . Encouraged by
the successful issue of the engagement of the first day, and in view of the valu-
able results that would ensue from the defeat of the army of General Meade, it
was thought advisable to renew the attack."*

FIRST DAY HIGHLIGHTS

Death of Major-General Reynolds

Major-General John Fulton Reynolds, killed at Gettysburg while commanding
the 1st Corps, was born in Lancaster, Pa., on the 21st day of September, 1820.
His father, John Reynolds, also a native of Lancaster County, was the son of
William Reynolds, who came to America in 1760 from Ireland. His mother's
maiden name was Lydia Moore, daughter of Samuel Moore, who held a commission
in the Revolutionary Army. He had an elder brother, William, who served as
Admiral in our Navy with great distinction, and also two other brothers who
served in the war, one as paymaster, and the other, the youngest of the four, as
Quartermaster-General of Pennsylvania.

William and John went first to an excellent school at Lititz, in Lancaster
County, going thence to Long Green, Md., and from there they returned to the
Lancaster Academy. Through the influence of James Buchanan, they received
appointments, one as midshipman in the Navy, and the other as cadet at West
Point. John was graduated from West Point on June 22nd, 1841, at the age of
twenty-one. He served with distinction during the Mexican War, and at the out-
break of the Civil War entered the Union Army. At the battle of Gaines' Mill, on
June 28th, 1862, he was captured, and after a confinement of six weeks in Libby
Prison, he was exchanged for General Barksdale.

General Reynolds was six feet tall, with dark hair and eyes. He was erect in
carriage and a superb horseman, so much at ease in the saddle as to be able to
pick a dime from the ground while riding at full speed. He was killed in the grove
now known as Reynolds' Grove on the morning of July 1st, between 10 and 11
o'clock, while directing the attack of Meredith's brigade against Archer's Confederate brigade. His body was first taken to the Seminary, and later to Lancaster,
where it was interred in the family graveyard.

The 26th Emergency Regiment

The 26th Emergency Regiment met the advance of Gordon's brigade of Early's
Division of Ewell's Corps in their advance into Gettysburg. Company A consisted
of students of the Lutheran Theological Seminary, Pennsylvania (now Gettysburg)
College, and citizens of the town. H. M. M. Richards, of Company A gives the
following sketch of the services of the regiment:

"Upon the first indication of an invasion of Pennsylvania, the 26th Regiment,
P. V. M., was organized and mustered into the United States service at Harrisburg,
under the command of Colonel W. W. Jennings of that city. Company A of this
regiment, to which I belonged, was composed of students from the Lutheran
Theological Seminary and the Pennsylvania College at Gettysburg, and of citizens
of the town; one other company came from Hanover, but a few miles distant.

"On June 23rd we left Harrisburg for Gettysburg, to be used, I believe, as
riflemen among the hills at or near Cashtown. A railroad accident prevented this

plan from being carried out, and kept us from reaching Gettysburg until the 2€ by which time General Early had reached Cashtown. In accordance with orc received from Major Granville O. Haller, acting aide-de-camp to General Cou commanding the Department of the Susquehanna, we were marched out on Chambersburg Pike at 10 A.M., June 26th, for a distance of about three and a l miles, accompanied by Major Robert Bell, who commanded a troop of horse, a raised, I understand, in Gettysburg. Having halted, our colonel, accompanied Major Bell, rode to the brow of an elevation and there saw General Early's tro a few miles distant.

"We, a few hundred men at most, were in the toils; what should be done? would gladly have marched to join the Army of the Potomac, under Meade, l where was it? Our colonel, left to his own resources, wisely decided to make effort to return to Harrisburg, and immediately struck off from the pike, the C federates capturing many of our rear-guard after a sharp skirmish, and send their cavalry in pursuit of us. These later overtook us in the afternoon at Witm house, about four and a half miles from Gettysburg on the Carlisle Road, wh after an engagement, they were repulsed with some loss. After many vicissitue we finally reached Harrisburg, having marched 54 out of 60 consecutive ho with a loss of some 200 men.

"It should be added that Gettysburg, small town as it was, had already furnisl its quota to the army. Moreover, on the first day of the battle, hundreds of unfortunate men of Reynolds's gallant corps were secreted, sheltered, fed, a aided in every way by the men and women of the town."

The First Soldier Killed at Gettysburg

George W. Sandoe, the first Union soldier killed at Gettysburg, was a mem of Company B Independent 21st Pennsylvania Cavalry. Upon arriving at Gett burg, June 26th, 1863, General Gordon sent out a picket line on the Baltimore P As these pickets reached the Nathaniel Lightner property, George W. Sandoe a William Lightner, also a member of Company B, approached the pike, com across the McAllister field from the direction of Rock Creek. Owing to a gro of bushes and trees along the fence, they did not discover the Confederate pick until they were ordered to halt. Lightner at once jumped his horse across the fe and escaped by riding rapidly down the pike. Sandoe's horse fell in making leap, and in attempting to escape by riding back in the direction from which came, Sandoe was shot. He lies buried at Mount Joy Church, in Mount J Adams County.

A Mysterious Letter

Having passed through Gettysburg on June 28th, General John B. Gordon Lee's army, went on to York and Wrightsville before returning on July 1st. In "Reminiscences of the Gettysburg Campaign" he tells the following story:

"We entered the city of York on Sunday morning. Halting on the main str where the sidewalks were densely packed, I rode a few rods in advance of my troc in order to speak to the people from my horse. As I checked him and turned full dust-begrimed face upon a bevy of ladies very near me, a cry of alarm ca from their midst; but after a few words of assurance from me, quiet and appar confidence were restored. I assured these ladies that the troops behind me, tho ill-clad and travel-stained, were good men and brave; that beneath their ro exteriors were hearts as loyal to women as ever beat in the breasts of honora men; that their own experience and the experience of their mothers, wives, a sisters at home had taught them how painful must be the sight of a hostile ar in their town; that under the orders of the Confederate commander-in-chief both private property and non-combatants were safe; that the spirit of vengeance and of rapine had no place in the bosoms of these dust-covered but knightly men; and I closed by pledging to York the head of any soldier under my command who destroyed private property, disturbed the repose of a single home, or insulted a woman.

"As we moved along the street after this episode, a little girl, probably twelve years of age, ran up to my horse and handed me a large bouquet of flowers in the center of which was a note in delicate handwriting, purporting to give the numbers and describe the position of the Union forces of Wrightsville, toward which I was advancing. I carefully read and reread this strange note. It bore no signature and contained no assurance of sympathy for the Southern cause, but it was so terse and explicit in its terms as to compel my confidence. The second day we were in front of Wrightsville, and from the high ridge on which this note suggested that I halt and examine the position of the Union troops, I eagerly scanned the prospect with my field-glasses, in order to verify the truth of the mysterious communication or detect its misrepresentations.

"There, in full view of us, was the town, just as described, nestling on the banks of the Susquehanna. There was the blue line of soldiers guarding the approach, drawn up, as indicated, along an intervening ridge and across the pike. There was the long bridge spanning the Susquehanna and connecting the town with Columbia on the other bank. Most important of all, there was the deep gorge or ravine running off to the right and extending around the left bank of the Federal line and to the river below the bridge. Not an inaccurate detail in that note could be discovered. I did not hesitate, therefore, to adopt its suggestion of moving down the gorge in order to throw my command on the flank, or possibly in the rear of the Union troops, and force them to a rapid retreat or surrender. The result of this movement vindicated the strategic wisdom of my unknown and—judging by the handwriting—woman correspondent, whose note was none the less martial because embedded in roses, and whose evident genius for war, had occasion offered, might have made her a captain equal to Catherine."

The Flag of the 16th Maine

A marker showing the position of the 16th Maine Infantry Regiment on the afternoon of the first day's battle stands at the intersection of Doubleday Avenue and the Mummasburg Road, and contains the following inscription:

POSITION HELD JULY 1, 1863, AT 4 O'CLOCK P.M.
BY THE 16TH MAINE INFANTRY
1ST BRIG., 2ND DIV., 1ST CORPS

WHILE THE REST OF THE DIVISION WAS RETIRING, THE
REGIMENT HAVING MOVED FROM THE POSITION AT THE
LEFT WHERE ITS MONUMENT STANDS, UNDER ORDERS
TO HOLD THIS POSITION AT ANY COST.

IT LOST ON THIS FIELD
KILLED 11, WOUNDED 62, CAPTURED 159
OUT OF 275 ENGAGED.

When almost surrounded, the regiment withdrew to the left of the railroad cut to help cover the withdrawal of Stewart's battery, which was also almost surrounded. The regiment had two flags, the Stars and Stripes and the flag of Maine.

Finally, assaulted by the flank and rear, they determined not to surrender their colors, but tore them from their staffs and into small bits, each man taking a star or a bit of silk which he placed in his pocket. Some of these fragments were carried through the southern prisons and finally home to Maine, where they are still treasured as precious relics by the relatives and friends of the brave men of the regiment.

The Barlow-Gordon Incident

Barlow's Knoll, a short distance northeast of Gettysburg, is named in honor of Brigadier-General Francis C. Barlow, in command of the 1st Division of the 11th Corps. In his "Reminiscences of the Civil War," General Gordon describes his meeting with Barlow:

"Returning from the banks of the Susquehanna, and meeting at Gettysburg, July 1, 1863, the advance of Lee's forces, my command was thrown quickly and squarely on the right flank of the Union Army. A more timely arrival never occurred. The battle had been raging for four or five hours. The Confederate General Archer, with a large part of his brigade, had been captured. Heth and Scales, Confederate generals, had been wounded. The ranking Union officer on the field, General Reynolds, had been killed, and General Hancock was assigned to command. The battle, upon the issue of which hung, perhaps, the fate of the Confederacy, was in full blast. The Union forces, at first driven back, now reënforced, were again advancing and pressing back Lee's left and threatening to envelop it. The Confederates were stubbornly contesting every foot of ground, but the Southern left was slowly yielding. A few moments more and the day's battle might have been ended by a complete turning of Lee's flank. I was ordered to move at once to the aid of the heavily pressed Confederates. With a ringing yell, my command rushed upon the line posted to protect the Union right. Here occurred a hand-to-hand struggle. That protecting Union line, once broken, left my command not only on the right flank, but obliquely in rear of it.

"Any troops that were ever marshalled would, under like conditions, have been as surely and swiftly shattered. Under the concentrated fire from front and flank, the marvel is that they escaped. In the midst of the wild disorder in his ranks, and through a storm of bullets, a Union officer was seeking to rally his men for a final stand. He, too, went down pierced by a minie ball. Riding forward with my rapidly advancing lines, I discovered that brave officer lying upon his back, with the July sun pouring its rays into his pale face. He was surrounded by the Union dead, and his own life seemed to be rapidly ebbing out. Quickly I dismounted and lifted his head. I gave him water from my canteen, and asked his name and the character of his wounds. He was Major-General Francis C. Barlow, of New York, and of Howard's Corps. The ball had entered his body in front and passed out near the spinal cord, paralyzing him in legs and arms. Neither of us had the remotest thought that he could survive many hours. I summoned several soldiers who were looking after the wounded, and directed them to place him upon a litter and carry him to the shade in the rear. Before parting, he asked me to take from his pocket a package of letters and destroy them. They were from his wife. He had one request to make of me. That request was that, if I lived to the end of the war and ever met Mrs. Barlow, I would tell her of our meeting on the field of Gettysburg and his thoughts of her in his last moments. He wished to assure me that he died doing his duty at the front, that he was willing to give his life for his country, and that his deepest regret was that he must die without looking upon her face again. I learned that Mrs. Barlow was with the Union Army, and near the battlefield. When it is remembered how closely Mrs. Gordon followed me, it will not be difficult to realize that my sympathies were especially stirred by the announcement that his wife was so near to him. Passing through the day's battle unhurt, I despatched, at its close, under a flag of truce, the promised message to Mrs. Barlow. I assured her that she should have safe escort to her husband's side.

"In the desperate encounters of the two succeeding days, and the retreat of Lee's army, I thought no more of Barlow, except to number him with the noble dead of the two armies who have so gloriously met their fate. The ball, however, had struck no vital point, and Barlow slowly recovered, though his fate was unknown to me. The following summer, in battles near Richmond, my kinsman with the same initials, General J. B. Gordon of North Carolina, was killed. Barlow, who had recovered, saw the announcement of his death, and entertained no doubt that he was the Gordon whom he had met on the field of Gettysburg. To me, therefore, Barlow was dead; to Barlow I was dead. Nearly fifteen years passed before either of us was undeceived. During my second term in the United States Senate, the Hon. Clarkson Potter of New York was the member of the House of Representatives. He invited me to dinner in Washington to meet a General Barlow who had served in the Union Army. Potter knew nothing of the Gettysburg incident. I had heard that there was another Barlow in the Union Army, and supposed of course, that it was this Barlow with whom I was to dine. Barlow had a similar reflection as to the Gordon he was to meet. Seated at Clarkson Potter's table, I asked Barlow: 'General, are you related to the Barlow who was killed at Gettysburg?' He replied: 'Why, I am the man, sir. Are you related to the Gordon who killed me?' 'I am the man, sir,' I responded. No words of mine can convey any conception of the emotions awakened by these startling announcements. Nothing short of an actual resurrection of the dead could have amazed either of us more. Thenceforward, until his untimely death in 1896, the friendship between us which was born amidst the thunders of Gettysburg was cherished by both."

General Ewell Is Hit by a Bullet

General Gordon gives an account of an amusing incident of the first day:

"Late in the afternoon of this first day's battle, when the firing had greatly decreased along most of the lines, General Ewell and I were riding through the streets of Gettysburg. In a previous battle he had lost one of his legs, but prided himself on the efficiency of the wooden one which he used in its place. As we rode together, a body of Union soldiers, posted behind some dwellings and fences on the outskirts of the town, suddenly opened a brisk fire. A number of Confederates were killed or wounded, and I heard the ominous thud of a minie ball as it struck General Ewell at my side. I quickly asked: 'Are you hurt, sir?' 'No, no,' he replied; 'I'm not hurt. But suppose that ball had struck you: we would have had the trouble of carrying you off the field, sir. You see how much better fixed I am for a fight than you are. It don't hurt a bit to be shot in a wooden leg.'

"Ewell was a most interesting and eccentric character. It is said that in his early manhood he had been disappointed in a love affair, and had never fully recovered from its effects. The fair maiden to whom he had given his affections had married another man; but Ewell, like the truest of knights, carried her image in his heart through long years. When he was promoted to the rank of brigadier or major-general, he evidenced the constancy of his affections by placing upon his staff the son of the woman whom he had loved in his youth. The meddlesome Fates, who seem to revel in the romances of lovers, had decreed that Ewell should be shot in battle and become the object of solicitude and tender nursing by this lady, Mrs. Brown, who had been for many years a widow. Her gentle ministrations soothed his weary weeks of suffering, a marriage ensued, and with it came the realization of Ewell's long-deferred hope. He was a most devoted husband. He never seemed to realize, however, that marriage had changed her name, for he proudly presented her to his friends as 'My wife, Mrs. Brown, sir.' "

[21]

The School Teachers' Regiment

The 151st Pennsylvania Infantry, commanded by Lieutenant-Colonel George F. McFarland, included Company D, made up mainly of the instructors and students of the Lost Creek Academy, of McAlisterville, Juniata County, of which Colonel McFarland was principal. For this reason it was called the "Schoolteachers' Regiment." The material throughout was excellent, many of the men being experienced marksmen. The regiment went into battle with 21 officers and 446 men, and sustained a loss in killed, wounded, and missing of 337, or over 75 per cent.

The casualties of the 26th North Carolina Regiment, against which they were engaged, were 588 out of 800, just about the same percentage.

Colonel McFarland lost his right leg and had the left permanently disabled, but survived until 1891. On the twenty-fifth anniversary of the battle, he delivered the dedicatory address at the unveiling of the regimental monument, exactly twenty-five years to the hour after his engagement in battle.

An Incident of the First Day

An incident, similar to that described by Browning in his poem "An Incident of the French Camp," occurred at the railroad cut early on the first day.

An officer of the 6th Wisconsin Regiment, active in the capture of the Mississippians belonging to the 2nd and 42nd Regiments, who had taken shelter in the railroad cut after turning the right of Cutler's line, approached Colonel Rufus R. Dawes after the engagement was over. Colonel Dawes supposed, from the erect appearance of the man, that he had come for further orders, but his compressed lips told a different story. With great effort the officer said: "Tell them at home I died like a man and a soldier." He then opened his coat, showed a ghastly wound on his breast, and dropped dead.

DORMITORY OF GETTYSBURG COLLEGE.—The dormitory of Gettysburg (then Pennsylvania) College sheltered many Union and Confederate wounded

THE SECOND DAY

THE scene of the engagements of the second and third days shifted to the south and southeast of Gettysburg. General Meade arrived on the field from his headquarters at Taneytown, Md., at 1 A.M., July 2nd, and established his headquarters at the Leister House, on the Taneytown Road, in rear of the line of the 2nd Corps. As soon as it was light he inspected the position already occupied and made arrangements for posting the several corps as they should reach the ground.

THE UNION LINE OF BATTLE.

Starting on the right with Slocum's 12th Corps, Williams' Division extended from Rock Creek by way of Spangler's Spring to Culp's Hill, with Geary's Division on the hill. The line between Culp's Hill and Cemetery Hill was held by Wadsworth's Division of the 1st Corps. Barlow's Division of the 11th Corps under Ames was located at the foot of East Cemetery Hill. Carman, Colgrove, Slocum, Geary, and Wainwright avenues follow these lines of battle.

On Cemetery Hill, across the Baltimore Pike, the line was held by Schurz and on his left Steinwehr, both of the 11th Corps. Robinson's Division of the 1st Corps extended across the Taneytown Road to Ziegler's Grove. Beyond lay Hancock's 2nd Corps, with the Divisions of Hays, Gibbon, and Caldwell from right to left. To the left of Hancock, Sickles' 3rd Corps, consisting of the Divisions of Humphreys and Birney, prolonged the line to the vicinity of Little Round Top. Beginning at the Taneytown Road, Hancock and Sedgwick avenues follow these lines of battle.

Arriving later in the day, the 5th Corps, under General Sykes, was posted on the Baltimore Pike, at the Rock Creek crossing. Later it occupied the ground about Round Top to the left of the 3rd Corps. The 6th Corps, under General Sedgwick, reaching the field still later after a march of over 30 miles, was posted in reserve back of Round Top, from which position portions were moved as circumstances demanded. The lines held by the 5th and 6th Corps coincide with Sykes, Ayres, Wright, and Howe Avenues.

STEVENS' KNOLL.—Arriving on Stevens' Knoll at the end of the first day,
General Slocum brought supporting troops. The lunettes
protecting the cannon remain intact.

Gamble's and Devin's brigades of Buford's Cavalry, which had
had an active part in the battle of the first day, were on the left
between Cemetery and Seminary Ridges until 10 A.M. when they
were ordered, by some mistake, to move to Westminster, Md.,
before the arrival of Gregg's Division on its way from Hanover,
and Merritt's brigade of Buford's Division from Mechanicsburg
(now Thurmont), Md.

General Meade's line, shaped like a fishhook, was about 3 miles
long. The right faced east, the center over Cemetery Hill, north,
and the left from Cemetery Hill to Round Top nearly west. The
whole line was supported by artillery brigades belonging to the
different corps.

CONFEDERATE LINE OF BATTLE.

General Lee's line was nearly the same shape as General Meade's
but, being the outer line, was about 6 miles long. On the right,
facing the two Round Tops, were Hood's and McLaws' Divisions
of Longstreet's Corps. On the left of McLaws, extending along
the line of Seminary Ridge, were the Divisions of Anderson and
Pender of Hill's Corps, with Heth's Division in the rear in reserve.
On the left of Pender, extending through the town along the line
of West Middle Street, was Rodes' Division of Ewell's Corps, then
Early's and Johnson's Divisions, the latter reaching to Benner's

Hill, east of Rock Creek. Pickett's Division of Longstreet's Corps was at Chambersburg, guarding trains, and Law's Brigade of Hood's Division of Longstreet's Corps at New Guilford, guarding the rear. The latter arrived at noon on the 2nd in time to participate in the day's engagement. Pickett's Division arrived later and was not engaged until the afternoon of the 3rd. The artillery was posted according to the different corps to which it was attached.

General Lee's line coincides with the present West Confederate Avenue along Seminary and Warfield or Snyder Ridges, west of the town, then runs through the town to coincide with East Confederate Avenue. The distance between the Union and Confederate lines is three-fourths of a mile to a mile.

Military critics agree that General Meade held the stronger position. Both flanks presented precipitous and rocky fronts, difficult to attack, and it was possible to send reinforcements by short distances from point to point.

SICKLES' CHANGE OF LINE.

As already stated, General Sickles' 3rd Corps was on the left of General Hancock's 2nd Corps on Cemetery Ridge, and Birney's Division was near the base of Little Round Top, replacing Geary's Division after its withdrawal to be posted on Culp's Hill. Humphreys' Division was on lów ground to the right between Cemetery Ridge and the Emmitsburg Road.

Anxious to know what was in his front, Sickles sent the Berdan Sharpshooters and the 3rd Maine Infantry forward on a reconnaissance. On reaching the Pitzer Woods, beyond the Emmitsburg Road, they found the Confederates there in force, and after a sharp engagement with Wilcox's Brigade, withdrew and reported.

Believing that Lee planned a flank movement on his line, and that the Emmitsburg Road afforded better positions for the artillery, Sickles moved his Corps forward and posted Humphreys' Division on the right along the Emmitsburg Road and his left extending to the Peach Orchard. Birney's Division prolonged the line from the Peach Orchard across the Wheatfield to Devil's Den. This new line formed a salient at the Peach Orchard and therefore presented two fronts, one to the west, the other to the south.

About 3 P.M. Sickles was called to General Meade's headquarters to a conference of corps commanders. Upon the sound of artillery, the conference adjourned, and Meade, Sickles, and Warren, Meade's Chief Engineer, rode to inspect Sickles' change of line. The artillery was already engaged, and believing it too late to make any changes since the enemy was present, Meade decided to attempt to hold the new position by sending in supports. After reviewing the new line, General Warren left the other members of the party and rode up Little Round Top. He found the height unoccupied except by the personnel of a signal station.

GENERAL MEADE'S STATUE.—General Meade viewed Pickett's Charge from the center of the Union line. This statue, like those of Reynolds and Sedgwick, is the work of Henry K. Bush-Brown.

GENERAL LEE'S PLAN.

Lee as well as Meade occupied the forenoon in the arrangement of his line of battle. After a conference with Ewell, he decided to attack Meade's left. In his report, Lee says:

"It was determined to make the principal attack upon the enemy's left, and endeavor to gain a position from which it was thought that our artillery could be brought to bear with effect. Longstreet was directed to place the division of McLaws and Hood on the right of Hill, partially enveloping the enemy's left, which he was to drive in.

"General Hill was ordered to threaten the enemy's center to prevent reinforcements being drawn to either wing, and coöperate with his right division in Longstreet's attack.

"General Ewell was instructed to make a simultaneous demonstration upon the enemy's right, to be converted into a real attack should opportunity offer."

When General Lee arranged this plan of attack he believed Meade's left terminated at the Peach Orchard; he did not know that Sickles' advance line extended to the left from the salient at the Peach Orchard to Devil's Den. In plain view of the Union signal station on Little Round Top, some of his forces were compelled to make a wide detour via the Black Horse Tavern on the Fairfield Road in order to avoid observation.

LITTLE ROUND TOP.

Meanwhile, General Warren on Little Round Top saw the importance of the hill as a tactical position on Meade's left. The signal officers were preparing to leave; he ordered them to remain and to keep waving their flags so as to lead the Confederates to believe that the hill was occupied. He dispatched a messenger to Devil's Den, where a Union battery was posted, with an order that a shot be fired to produce confusion in the woods in front, through which Hood's forces were supposed to be advancing. Seeing the reflection of the sunlight from Confederate muskets, he realized that if this important position were to be held, it would be necessary to get troops there without delay.

Quickly he sent a member of his staff to Sickles for troops. Sickles said none could be spared. Warren sent another staff officer to Meade, who immediately ordered Sykes to move his Corps to Little Round Top. Barnes' Division of this Corps had already been called for by Sickles to defend his line, and three brigades, Vincent's, Tilton's, and Sweitzer's, were moving toward the Wheatfield. Learning of the need of troops on Little Round Top, Vincent moved back, skirted the east side of Little Round Top, and went into position between Little and Big Round Top, arriving just before the Confederates from Hood's right advanced over Big Round Top.

Having watched these movements, Warren rode down to the crossing of what is now Sykes Avenue and the Wheatfield Road. There he met Colonel O'Rorke, in command of the 140th New York, and ordered his regiment, together with Hazlett's battery, to the crest of the hill. With the addition of Weed's Brigade, the combined forces held the Round Tops. There was a desperate engagement in which both contestants displayed courage of a very high order. The Union soldiers were victorious, and Meade's left was secured against further attack.

THE PEACH ORCHARD AND THE WHEATFIELD.

After the struggle for the possession of Little Round Top, the other Confederate brigades of Hood and McLaws advanced rapidly. A lack of coordination in their movement allowed Meade to bring up supports. Three brigades of Anderson's Division of Hill's Corps advanced against Humphreys' line, in the following order: Wilcox, Perry, Wright. Wounded, General Pender was unable to direct Posey and Mahone in support of Wright, and Wright was obliged to withdraw. Humphreys was compelled to change front in order to meet the assault on his flanks. This maneuver served to stay the Confederate attack for a brief time. The Valley of Death between the Round Tops and the opposite height was now a seething mass of opposing forces, enshrouded in clouds of smoke.

Meade had already depleted his right to support his left by withdrawing all of Slocum's 12th Corps except Greene's Brigade. He now sent all of the 5th Corps to the left and ordered Caldwell's Division from the left of Hancock's 2nd Corps south of the Angle to the Wheatfield. Willard's Brigade on Hays' line of the 2nd Corps was ordered to advance and oppose the Confederate, Barksdale, who, after crossing the Emmitsburg Road north of the Peach Orchard and the field beyond, reached Watson's Union battery posted on the Trostle farm. General Sickles was severely and Barksdale mortally wounded.

Wofford's Brigade of McLaws' Division broke through the salient at the Peach Orchard and reached the valley between Devil's Den and Little Round Top, where they were met by a charge of the Pennsylvania Reserves of Crawford's Division, led by McCandless, some of whose men fought in sight of their own homes. Wofford was obliged to withdraw to and beyond the Wheatfield; the Reserves advanced across the valley from their position

WHEATFIELD.—Scene of carnage on the second day

on the north of Little Round Top and reached the stone wall on the east side of the Wheatfield. Here they remained until after Pickett's charge on the 3rd, when they advanced against the Confederates who had succeeded in regaining control of that part of the field.

About the time when Sickles was wounded, Meade directed Hancock to assume command of Sickles' Corps in addition to his own. Meade in person led Lockwood's brigade, brought from the extreme right, against the Confederate advance. Newton, now in command of the 1st Corps, sent in Doubleday's Division. With these troops Hancock checked the advance of the Confererate brigades of Barksdale, Wilcox, Perry, and Wright, while Sykes checked the advance of Hood and McLaws. Brigades of the 6th Corps reached the field toward the close of the engagement. Withdrawing from the Wheatfield Road, Bigelow's battery made a determined stand at the Trostle buildings and succeeded in checking the Confederate advance until the gap on Sickles' first line was protected by a line of guns. Most of the Confederate brigades got no farther than Plum Run, except Wright's, which actually reached the line of guns on Hancock's front before it was obliged to withdraw.

During the repulse of the Confederate advance, the 1st Minnesota regiment of Harrow's· Brigade of Gibbon's Division of Hancock's Corps was ordered by Hancock to oppose Wilcox's and Perry's Brigades, rapidly advancing against Hancock's left. The Minnesota regiment moved up at once and succeeded in repelling the attack, but only after losing 82 per cent of its men.

Though seriously threatened, Meade's line held, and after the repulse of Wright, the attack ended. During the night the line was prolonged to the top of Big Round Top. The Confederates remained west of Plum Run, except at Big Round Top, where they intrenched along the western slope.

Ewell's Attack on Meade's Right.

Ordered by Lee to begin his attack on Meade's right at the same time as Longstreet's attack on Meade's left, Ewell's artillery on Benner's Hill opened fire on Culp's Hill and Cemetery Hill where the Union forces were posted and well protected with earthworks. On account of the destructive fire from the

Union batteries on East Cemetery Hill, Ewell lost most of his guns, and no infantry advance was made until Longstreet's assault had ended. At sundown General Johnson's infantry advanced against Culp's Hill, General Early against East Cemetery Hill. Rodes, who was directed to move against West Cemetery Hill, was unable to obey instructions. General Walker, who had been sent east to Brinkerhoff Ridge in the forenoon, to guard Ewell's flank, and who was expected to assist in this attack, was prevented by meeting part of the Union cavalry of Gregg's Division that had arrived via Hanover on the forenoon of the 2nd. After an engagement with Gregg, Walker moved up to assist Johnson, but too late to be of service, as the attack on Culp's Hill had ended.

MONUMENT OF THE IRISH BRIGADE.—
At the foot of the Celtic Cross is the Irish wolfhound, symbolic of devotion.

The attack was conducted with the greatest dash and daring, in part up rough slopes of woodland over heaped boulders. On East Cemetery Hill the fight among the Union guns was hand to hand, and clubbed muskets, stones, and rammers were used to drive back the assailants. After sunset a bright moon illuminated the field. The Union troops stood firm, and at 10 o'clock the Confederates desisted, having captured only a few Union entrenchments.

SITUATION AT END OF THE SECOND DAY.

Lee's assaults on Meade's left had failed to accomplish anything decisive. While Sickles' advance-line was driven back and most of the field, including the Peach Orchard, the Wheatfield, Devil's Den, and the base of Big Round Top, was occupied by the Confederates, Meade's line was practically intact from the crest of Big Round Top on the left to near Spangler's Spring on the right. On the slopes of Round Top, on Cemetery Hill and Culp's Hill, the advantage of the defensive positions multiplied the forces of the defenders in comparison with the attackers at least three to one. Prodigious deeds of valor were performed by both armies, and courage of the highest order was displayed in attack and in the defense. Casualties were very heavy on both sides. Meade estimated that his losses were 65 per cent of the total for the three days. At the end of the day he made the following report:

"July 2, 1863, 8 P.M. The enemy attacked me about 4 P.M. this day, and, after one of the severest contests of the war, was repulsed at all points. We have suffered considerably in killed and wounded. Among the former are Brigadier Generals Paul and Zook, and among the wounded are Generals Sickles, Barlow, Graham, and Warren slightly. We have taken a large number of prisoners. I shall remain in my present position tomorrow, but am not prepared to say, until better advised of the condition of the army, whether my operations will be of an offensive or defensive character."

Later in the night, at a council of war held by Meade with his corps commanders—Gibbon, Williams, Sykes, Newton, Howard, Hancock, Sedgwick and Slocum—sentiment favored remaining and fighting a defensive battle. As Lee attacked both wings of Meade's line on the 2nd it was expected that if another attack were made it would be on the center. This expectation was correct—Wright's attack on the 2nd, when he succeeded in reaching Meade's line south of the Angle, led Lee to believe that this was the most vulnerable point.

General Lee had more definite plans:

"The result of this day's operations induced the belief that, with proper concert of action, and with the increased support that the positions gained on the right would enable the artillery to render the assaulting column, we should ultimately succeed, and it was accordingly determined to continue the attack."

The general plan was unchanged. Longstreet, re-enforced by Pickett's three brigades, which arrived near the battlefield during the afternoon of the 2nd, was ordered to attack the next morning, and General Ewell was directed to assail the enemy's right at the same time. The latter, during the night, re-enforced General Johnson with three brigades from Rodes' and Early's Divisions.

[31]

INCIDENTS OF THE SECOND DAY

The Roger House

The Roger House is located on the west side of the Emmitsburg Road, about a mile south of Gettysburg, midway between Meade's line of battle on Cemetery Ridge and Lee's line on Seminary Ridge. On the afternoon of July 2nd, after Sickles advanced his corps from its first position to the Emmitsburg Road, it was surrounded by the right of the new line. The 1st Massachusetts Regiment, whose monument stands adjacent to the house, held this part of the line, and was hotly engaged when the brigades of Wilcox and Wright advanced during the assault of Longstreet on the Union left on the afternoon of the 2nd. During Pickett's Charge, on the afternoon of the 3rd, the house was again surrounded by fighting men.

While the battle raged on all sides, a granddaughter of the owner, Miss Josephine Miller, remained, and, notwithstanding the great danger, baked bread and biscuits for the hungry soldiers. In 1896, Miss Miller, then Mrs. Slyder, paid a visit to her old home, and related the following story of her experience to Mr. Wilfred Pearse, of Boston, Mass., a visitor to Gettysburg at the same time. After his return he published the following article.

"The veterans of the 1st Massachusetts Infantry Regiment will be glad to learn that the only woman member of the 3rd Army Corps 'Veterans' Association,' Mrs. Slyder, née Miss Josephine Miller, granddaughter of farmer Roger, owner of the farm near which the 1st Massachusetts monument stands, is visiting her old home on the battleground where she stood from sunrise to sunset for two days of the battle making hot biscuits for the Boys in Blue. She refused to take money for the bread, and refused to stop her work even when Confederate shells were bursting around the house. She told me the other day that when her stock of flour was almost exhausted six members of the 1st Massachusetts kindly volunteered to go out and steal three sacks of flour from General Sickles' commissary stores. In an hour's time they returned with flour, raisins, currants, and a whole sheep, with which a rattling good meal was made.

"The old range still stands in the kitchen, and in it, at the last reunion of the 3rd Corps, Mrs. Slyder cooked a dinner for General Sickles."

Spangler's Spring

This spring, which takes its name from Abraham Spangler, its owner at the time of the battle, is located at the southeast corner of Culp's Hill. Inasmuch as it was used by soldiers of both armies during the battle, and since then by thousands of tourists, it is an interesting feature of the field. Only during the drought of 1930 has it failed to send forth a copious flow of cool, pure water. At the time of the battle it was surrounded by a wall of flat stones with a flagstone cover over the top. These were removed and a canopy top erected.

The 12th Corps of the Army of the Potomac occupied this part of Meade's line on the night of the first day and until the afternoon of the 2nd, when the troops were ordered to the left to help repel Longstreet's assault. Until this time the spring was used only by the Union troops. During their absence, the Confederates under Johnson moved up and took possession of part of the vacated line. In the early morning of the third day, the Union forces, who had returned from the left during the night of the 2nd, attacked Johnson, drove him out and succeeded in regaining possession of the line that had been vacated by them on the afternoon of the 2nd, including the spring.

The story that a truce was entered into between the opposing forces on the night of the 2nd and that they met in large numbers at the spring to get water is a

SPANGLER'S SPRING.—Spangler's Spring was used first by the Union, then by the Confederate troops, and since by thousands of tourists

mistake. The captured and wounded of the Union forces were allowed access to it along with the Confederates who were there at the time, but there was no truce. When armies were encamped, pickets from the opposing lines would sometimes get together, usually to trade coffee and tobacco, but this was never done when a battle was in progress.

The following extract from the address of Captain Joseph Matchett at the dedication of the monument erected by the 46th Pennsylvania Infantry Regiment, shows that there was no truce:

"Some time in the night (2nd), we were ordered to return to our works on Culp's Hill. It seems Captain Selfridge of Company H had taken some of his men's canteens and gone ahead to Spangler's Spring to fill them, when he discovered 'Johnnies' also filling their canteens. He backed out with the best grace he could command, and reported it to the colonel. Colonel McDougall, the brigade commander, did not believe it and got very angry, but the colonel of the regiment insisted on deploying his men, and sent a skirmish line, who found the enemy as stated and saved many lives."

Colonel Avery's Lost Grave

Among those who faced death in the desperate charge on the Union right on East Cemetery Hill, July 2nd, Colonel I. E. Avery, of North Carolina, in command of Hoke's brigade, bore a gallant part. At the head of the column he led his men up the slope of Cemetery Hill and, a conspicuous mark, fell mortally wounded.

Unable to speak, he drew a card from his pocket and wrote the following: "Tell father that I died with my face toward the enemy." In the retreat from Gettysburg, his body was taken along to be delivered to his family, but when the army reached Williamsport the Potomac was too high to cross. There, in the cemetery overlooking the river, the remains were interred in an oak coffin under a pine tree. He was buried in his uniform by the men who saw him fall.

Thirty years after, Judge A. C. Avery, of the Supreme Court of North Carolina, a resident of Morgantown, and Captain J. A. McPherson of Fayette, N. C., both veterans of the Confederacy, came to Williamsport with the object of locating Colonel Avery's grave. Their search was fruitless.

The Leister House

On his arrival, General Meade established his headquarters at the Leister House, one of the oldest houses in the community, located at the intersection of Meade Avenue and the Taneytown Road. At the time of the battle it was the property of a widow, Mrs. Leister. It now belongs to the Government, and a bronze plate marks it as Meade's Headquarters. It is built of logs, chinked and weatherboarded with rough pine boards, pierced by bullet-holes and scarred by shells.

Inside there are two rooms, a small kitchen at the west, and a larger room at the east. In the latter, Meade held a council of war after the battle of the 2nd had ended, summoning his Corps commanders between 9 and 10 o'clock to consult them as to what action, if any, should be taken on the 3rd. Generals Sedgwick, Slocum, Hancock, Howard, Sykes, Newton, Birney, Williams, and Gibbon were present. The following questions were asked:

(1) Under existing circumstances is it advisable for this army to remain in its present position, or to retire to another nearer its base of supplies?

(2) It being determined to remain in present position, shall the army attack or wait the attack of the enemy?

(3) If we wait attack, how long?

Replies:

Gibbon: (1) Correct position of the army, but would not retreat. (2) In no condition to attack, in his opinion. (3) Until he moves.

Williams: (1) Stay. (2) Wait attack. (3) One day.

Birney and Sykes: Same as General Williams.

Newton: (1) Correct position of the army, but would not retreat. (2) By all means not attack. (3) If we wait it will give them a chance to cut our line.

Howard: (1) Remain. (2) Wait attack until 4 P.M. tomorrow. (3) If don't attack, attack them.

Hancock: (1) Rectify position without moving so as to give up field. (2) Not attack unless our communications are cut. (3) Can't wait long; can't be idle.

Sedgwick: (1) Remain. (2) Wait attack. (3) At least one day.

Slocum: (1) Stay and fight it out.

The unanimous opinion of the council was to stay and await attack. Just as the council broke up, General Meade said to Gibbon, "If Lee attacks tomorrow, it will be on your front. He has made attacks on both our flanks and failed, and if he concludes to try it again it will be on our center." The attack of Lee on the 3rd was made where Meade expected.

During the forenoon of the third day, conditions at headquarters were generally quiet. In the afternoon, when the Confederate artillery on Seminary Ridge opened fire as a prelude to Pickett's Charge, it was directed mainly against the left center of the Union line on Cemetery Ridge. As the location of Meade's headquarters was in the immediate rear, just under the crest of the ridge, much damage was done by the hail of shot and shell that crossed the ridge. A shell exploded in the yard among the staff officers' horses tied to the fence, and a number of them were killed, while still other horses were killed in the rear of the building. Several members of the headquarters' guard were slightly wounded.

George G. Meade, a grandson of General Meade, in his interesting narrative "With Meade at Gettysburg," tells the following story:

"During this rain of Confederate shell, and while Meade, deep in thought, was walking up and down this little back yard between the house and the Taneytown Road, he chanced to notice that some of his staff, during the enforced inactivity while waiting the pleasure of their general, were gradually and probably unconsciously edging around the side of the house.

" 'Gentlemen,' he said, stopping and smiling pleasantly, 'Are you trying to find a safer place? You remind me of the man who was driving the ox-cart which took ammunition for the heavy guns on the field of Palo Alto. Finding himself within range, he tilted up his cart and got behind it. Just then General Taylor came along, and seeing the attempt at shelter, shouted, "You damned fool; don't you know you are no safer there than anywhere else?" The driver replied, "I don't suppose I am, General, but it kind o' feels so." ' "

As the firing still continued it was decided to move the headquarters several hundred yards south on the Taneytown Road, to a barn on the Cassatt property. There a Confederate shell exploded and wounded General Butterfield, the chief of staff, who was obliged to leave the field and was unable to return that day. After remaining a short time, General Meade and staff removed to General Slocum's headquarters at Powers' Hill, along the Baltimore Pike, moving there by way of Granite Lane.

The Louisiana Tigers

Major Chatham R. Wheat's battalion of Louisiana Infantry was organized in New Orleans in May, 1861. Their first engagement was in the first battle of Bull Run, where Major Wheat was shot through both lungs. After his recovery, he re-entered the service and took an active part in command of the battalion in the defense of Richmond in 1863 against the advance of the Union forces under McClellan. During this campaign the battalion became known as "The Louisiana Tigers" on account of their desperate fighting qualities. At the battle of Gaines Mill, Major Wheat and several other leading officers of the battalion were killed, and the loss of the organization was very heavy. It was then broken up and the survivors distributed among the other Louisiana regiments, of Hays' brigade of Early's Division, and Nicholls' brigade of Johnson's Division of Ewell's Corps. A number of them were in the battle of Gettysburg with these brigades, but not as the separate organization originally known as "The Louisiana Tigers." This designation was given to all the Louisiana troops after the original battalion was discontinued. The story sometimes told, that 1,700 Louisiana Tigers attacked East Cemetery Hill on July 2nd, that all but 300 were killed or captured, and that the organization was unknown afterward, is not correct.

General Mead's "Baldy"

In the first great battle of the Civil War, at Bull Run, there was a bright bay horse with white face and feet. He, as well as his rider, was seriously wounded and the horse was turned back to the quartermaster to recover. In September General Meade bought him and named him "Baldy." Meade became deeply attached to the horse but his staff officers soon began to complain of his peculiar racking gait which was hard to follow. Faster than a walk and slow for a trot, it compelled the staff alternately to trot and walk.

"Baldy" was wounded twice at the first battle of Bull Run; he was at the battle of Drainsville; he took part in two of the seven days' fighting around Richmond in the summer of 1862; he carried his master at Groveton, August 29th; at the second battle of Bull Run; at South Mountain and at Antietam. In the last battle he was left on the field for dead, but in the next Federal advance he was discovered quietly grazing on the battleground with a deep wound in his neck. He was tenderly cared for and soon was fit for duty. He bore the general at the battles of Fredericksburg and Chancellorsville. For two days he was present at Gettysburg, where he received his most grievous wound from a bullet entering his body between the ribs and lodging there. Meade would not part with his and kept him with the army until the following spring.

In the preparations of the Army of the Potomac for the last campaign, "Baldy" was sent to pasture at Downingtown, Pa. After the surrender of Lee at Appomattox,

Meade hurried to Philadelphia where he again met his faithful charger, fully recovered. For many years the horse and the general were inseparable companions, and when Meade died in 1872, "Baldy" followed the hearse. Ten years later he died, and his head and two fore-hoofs were mounted and are now cherished relics of the George G. Meade Post, Grand Army of the Republic, in Philadelphia.

General Lee's "Traveller"

The most famous of the steeds in the stables of General Lee, was "Traveller," an iron-gray horse. He was raised in Greenbriar County, Virginia, near Blue Sulphur Springs, and as a colt won first prize at a fair in Lewisburg. When hostilities commenced, Traveller, then called "Jeff Davis," was owned by Major Thomas L. Broun, who had paid $175 in gold for him. In the spring of 1862, Lee bought him for $200 and changed his name to "Traveller."

"Traveller" was the especial companion of the general. His fine proportions attracted immediate attention. He was gray in color, with black points, a long mane, and flowing tail. He stood sixteen hands high, and was five years old in the spring of 1862. His figure was muscular, with deep chest and short back, strong haunches, flat legs, small head, quick eyes, broad forehead, and small feet. His rapid, springy step and bold carriage made him conspicuous. On a long and tedious march he easily carried Lee's weight at five or six miles an hour without faltering and at the end of the day's march seemed to be as fresh as at the beginning. The other horses broke down under the strain and each in turn proved unequal to the rigors of war, but "Traveller" sturdily withstood the hardships of the campaigns in Virginia, Maryland, and Pennsylvania. When, in April, 1865, the last battle of the Army of Northern Virginia had been fought and Lee rode to the McLean House at Appomattox Court House, he was astride "Traveller" who carried him back to his waiting army, and then to Richmond. When Lee became a private citizen and retired to Washington and Lee University as its president, the veteran war-horse was still with him, and as the years passed and both master and servant neared life's ending, they became more closely attached. As the funeral cortege accompanied Lee to his last resting-place, "Traveller" marched behind the hearse. After "Traveller's" death, his skeleton was mounted and is on exhibition in the museum in the chapel on the campus of Washington and Lee University.

A Union Battery, in action on the afternoon of the second day

THE THIRD DAY

THE first engagement on the third day was a continuation and conclusion of the attack and defense of Meade's right. His forces, returning from the left, where they had been sent on the afternoon of the 2nd, found part of their earthworks in possession of the enemy. At daybreak preparations were made to recapture the lost entrenchments. By 10.30 the effort was successful, and Meade's line was once more intact from end to end.

SECOND BATTLE AT CULP'S HILL.

This action on the morning of the 3rd was one of the most hotly contested of the battle. The Confederate losses in killed were almost the same as those of Pickett's Division in the attack on Meade's left center in the afternoon. Meade's losses were comparatively light, as his line was well protected by the line of earthworks. So intense was the artillery and musketry fire that hundreds of trees were shattered. After the repulse, Johnson's forces were withdrawn, and this ended their participation in the battle.

MEADE'S LINE OF THE THIRD DAY.

After the engagement on the morning of the 2nd, the 12th Corps reoccupied its original line, beginning on the right at Spangler's Hill and extending to and over Culp's Hill. Wadsworth's Division of the 1st Corps retained its position of the 2nd, between Culp's Hill and Barlow's Division under Ames of the 11th Corps, at the foot of East Cemetery Hill. Barlow's Division was strengthened by a brigade of the 2nd Corps. Doubleday's Division of the 1st Corps, which had taken the position of Caldwell's Division on the left of the 2nd Corps, remained. Caldwell was posted so as to support the artillery reserve to the left of Doubleday.

The other divisions of the 1st and 2nd Corps remained in the positions they occupied on the morning of the 2nd. The 5th Corps extended the line from the left of the artillery reserve to Big Round Top. Some of the brigades of the 6th Corps were put in position as local reserves and others to protect the flanks of the line. The 3rd Corps was posted in rear of the center as a general

MEADE'S HEADQUARTERS.—The Leister House, General Meade's headquarters until the artillery fire on the third day compelled him to move

reserve. A detachment of cavalry was in reserve in rear of the 2nd Corps at the Angle. Few changes were made in the artillery positions. Beginning at Cemetery Hill and extending to Little Round Top, about ninety guns, under General Hunt, were in position to operate.

LEE'S LINE OF THE THIRD DAY.

Beginning on the right, Longstreet's Corps held the ground west of Plum Run, including the base of Big Round Top, Devil's Den, and the Peach Orchard. Pickett's Division, after its arrival on the field on the morning of the 3rd, took the place of Anderson in reserve. Heth's and Pender's Divisions extended the line to the left on Seminary Ridge, connecting with part of Rodes' Division in the western part of the town. Early's and Johnson's Divisions, after the engagement on the morning of the 3rd, held their positions of the 2nd. Changes in the positions of the batteries of artillery were made on the morning of the 3rd. A total of 138 guns were in position to operate. Those on the right were in charge of Colonel E. P. Alexander; those on the left under Colonel R. L. Walker.

THE BLISS BUILDINGS.

After the end of the engagement at Culp's Hill at 10.30 A.M.

there was a short battle for the capture of the Bliss house and barn, midway between the lines in front of Ziegler's Grove. These buildings were occupied by Confederate sharpshooters, who were causing considerable loss in Hays' line of the 2nd Corps at the grove. Two regiments were sent forward, the 12th New Jersey and the 14th Connecticut, and the buildings were captured and burned.

THE ARTILLERY DUEL.

Until 1 o'clock there was comparative quiet. It was ended on the stroke of the hour by two guns of Miller's battery belonging to the Washington artillery of New Orleans, posted near the Peach Orchard, and fired in rapid succession as a signal to the Confederate artillery.

The Confederate Colonel Alexander says:

"*At exactly 1 o'clock by my watch the two signal guns were heard in quick succession. In another minute every gun was at work. The enemy was not slow in coming back at us, and the grand roar of nearly the whole of both armies burst in on the silence.*

"*The enemy's position seemed to have broken out with guns everywhere, and from Round Top to Cemetery Hill was blazing like a volcano.*"

The artillery duel was but a preface, intended to clear the ground for the infantry action to follow. The order had already been given by Longstreet to Alexander:

"*Colonel: The intention is to advance the infantry if the artillery has the desired effect of driving the enemy off, or having other effect such as to warrant us in making the attack. When the moment arrives advise General Pickett, and of course advance such artillery as you can use in making the attack.*"

General Wright, who was present when this order was received, expressed doubt as to whether the attack could be successfully made. He said:

"*It is not so hard to go there as it looks; I was nearly there with my brigade yesterday. The trouble is to stay there. The whole Yankee army is there in a bunch.*"

For one and a half hours the air was filled with screaming, whistling shot and shell. An occasional Whitworth missile, from Oak Hill on the north, made, on account of its peculiar form, a noise that could be heard above the din of all others. The headquarters of General Meade at the Leister House formed a concentric

EISENHOWER HISTORIC SITE NOW OPEN
AT GETTYSBURG

When America engaged in World War I, a then 28-year old Captain Dwight David Eisenhower was ordered to proceed to Gettysburg, PA to train the new American Tank Corps. Eisenhower was the only regular military officer assigned to the 5600 troops at Gettysburg, so the responsibilities were enormous. Nonetheless, he attacked his assignment with initiative and zeal and in time he became known as the father of the American Tank Corps. His superb ability to train troops to use the new "iron monsters" won him the Distinguished Service Medal for his Gettysburg accomplishments.

The training center, known as Camp Colt, was constructed within the Gettysburg National Military Park where Pickett's Charge occurred in 1863. Millions have gazed across those peaceful rolling fields where Pickett's 15,000 made their charge into history. But few visitors chance upon the small plaque within those fields that reads: "This spot marks the site of Camp Colt, the birthplace of the Tank Corps of the United States Army in the spring of 1918."

Following World War I, Camp Colt was de-activated and Ike left with his tankers, not to return to Gettysburg until after World War II. From a young captain at Gettysburg, he went on to become Supreme Commander of Allied

Forces in Europe, a Five Star General, the first Commander of the International Army of NATO, Chairman of the Joint Chiefs of Staff, President of Columbia University, and a two-term President of the United States.

Although Eisenhower had accomplished as much as any man could in one lifetime, another desire stirred within him. Ike confessed on several occasions that, "I always wanted a spot of ground to put in better shape than it was when I purchased it." And so, in 1952, Ike and Mamie returned to Gettysburg, bought a farm, and began to build up the land. His retirement years began on January 20th, 1961.

The Eisenhowers lived in 37 places in 35 years but only ever called one place home. The white gates to their 495 acre country estate opened to the public on Flag Day, June 14th, 1980, when the U.S. National Park Service unveiled the Eisenhower National Historic Site at Gettysburg.

Visitors to the country estate find a modified Georgian home with the 15 rooms preserved and protected by the interpretive staff of the U.S. National Park Service.

point continually swept with a storm of shot and shell. Headquarters were therefore moved to Slocum's headquarters at Powers' Hill, along the Baltimore Pike.

Batteries on the Union line, especially at the Angle, were badly damaged, and General Hunt had others brought forward with additional supplies of ammunition. On the whole the losses inflicted upon the Union infantry were comparatively light. The stone wall and the undulations of the ground afforded protection, as most of the men were lying down.

After the artillery had operated for about an hour and a half, Meade and Hunt deemed it prudent to stop the fire, in order to cool the guns, save ammunition, and allow the atmosphere between the lines to clear of the dense cloud of smoke before the expected attack was made. This pause in the fire led the Confederates to believe that the Union line was demoralized, and that the opportune time had arrived for the onset of the infantry. Accordingly, they moved forward and Pickett's Charge was on.

At the signal station on Little Round Top, General Warren and others saw gray infantry moving out across the plain in front of the Spangler Woods. Warren at once wig-wagged to General Hunt:

"They are moving out to attack."

DEVIL'S DEN.—Hid among the rocks of Devil's Den, Confederate sharpshooters picked off officers and men occupying Little Round Top

This message was passed from man to man along the entire Union line.

Pickett's Charge.

Pickett's Division of Longstreet's Corps was moved from the rear to the ravine in front of the Spangler Woods and placed in line as follows: Kemper on the right; Garnett on the left in the front line; Armistead in the rear, overlapping Kemper's left and Garnett's right, in the second line. On the left of Garnett was ranged Archer's Brigade of Hill's Corps under Frye, then Pettigrew's Brigade under Marshall. Next to Marshall came Davis' Brigade of Hill's Corps, and on the extreme left Brockenbrough's Brigade, also of Hill's Corps. In the rear of the right of Pickett were the brigades of Wilcox and Perry of Hill's Corps and in the rear of Pettigrew were the brigades of Scales and Lane of Hill's Corps, in command of Trimble.

The column of assault consisted of 42 regiments—19 Virginia, 15 North Carolina, 2 Alabama, 3 Tennessee, and 3 Mississippi—a total of about 15,000 men.

In addition to the artillery fire, they encountered 27 regiments—9 of New York, 5 of Pennsylvania, 3 of Massachusetts, 3 of Vermont, 1 of Michigan, 1 of Maine, 1 of Minnesota, 1 of New Jersey, 1 of Connecticut, 1 of Ohio, and 1 of Delaware—a total of 9,000 to 10,000 men.

In advance of the assaulting column a strong skirmish line was deployed. A skirmish line was also deployed in front of Meade's line, which fell back as the assaulting column drew near.

The Advance.

General Longstreet ordered General Alexander, Chief of Artillery, to watch the havoc wrought in the Union line and signify the moment for advance.

General Alexander says:

"Before the cannonade opened I made up my mind to give the order to advance within fifteen or twenty minutes after it began. But when I looked at the full development of the enemy's batteries and knew that his infantry was generally protected from fire by stone walls and swells of the ground, I could not bring myself to give the word.

"I let the 15 minutes pass, and 20, and 25, hoping vainly for something to turn up. Then I wrote to Pickett: 'If you are coming at all, come at once,

or I cannot give you proper support; but the enemy's fire has not slackened at all; at least eighteen guns are still firing from the cemetery itself.'

"Five minutes after sending that message, the enemy's fire suddenly began to slacken, and the guns in the cemetery limbered up and vacated the position.

"Then I wrote to Pickett: 'Come quick; eighteen guns are gone; unless you advance quick, my ammunition won't let me support you properly.'

"Pickett then rode forward, and on meeting Longstreet said: 'General, shall I advance?' Longstreet nodded his assent and the column moved forward."

The column passed through the line of guns, fifteen or eighteen of which had been ordered to follow. Meanwhile the eighteen Union guns that were withdrawn were replaced by others. The Union line was once more intact, and it opened a terrific fire against the rapidly moving columns of assault. As the Confederates continued to advance, their courage unaffected in face of the tremendous fire of both artillery and infantry, their enemies were filled with admiration.

At the Emmitsburg Road, where post-and-rail fences had to be crossed, the line was broken, but only for a moment. The musketry fire from the Union line was so heavy that the attacking column was unable to maintain a regular alignment, and when the Angle was reached the identity of the different brigades was lost.

Armistead's Brigade forged to the front at the Angle, and, reaching the wall, Armistead raised his hat on his sword and said:

"Give them the cold steel, boys!"

With a few men he advanced to Cushing's guns, where he fell, mortally wounded. Cushing also was mortally wounded. Garnett, who was mounted, was killed a short distance from the wall. Kemper was badly wounded. Pickett lost all of his field officers but one. The Union Generals Hancock and Gibbon were wounded at the same time. For a short time the struggle was hand to hand.

To the right of the Angle most of the brigades on Pickett's left reached the stone wall on Hays' front at Ziegler's Grove, but were obliged to retreat after meeting a withering fire both in front and on flank.

The brigades of Wilcox and Perry, in the rear of Pickett's right, did not move until after the advance lines were part way across. Because of a misunderstanding, a gap was opened between Pickett's right and Wilcox's left. At once Stannard's Vermont Brigade of the 1st Corps attacked both Pickett's right and Wilcox's left.

WHITWORTH GUNS.—These two Whitworths, imported from England by the Confederates, were the only breech-loading guns used in the battle

General Pickett, who had reached the Codori buildings, saw that the assaulting forces were unable to accomplish the object of the charge, and ordered a retreat. It was accomplished, but with heavy losses.

Both commanding officers witnessed the retreat: General Meade from where his statue stands east of the Angle, and General Lee from the position of his statue north of the Spangler Woods.

ENGAGEMENTS ON THE UNION LEFT.

While Pickett's Charge was under way, the Pennsylvania Reserves, under McCandless, charged from the stone wall on the east side of the Wheatfield and regained possession of Devil's Den and adjacent territory held by Longstreet's forces since the engagement of the afternoon of the 2nd. Farther south, between Big Round Top and the line held by Longstreet's right, a cavalry charge was made by Farnsworth's Brigade of Kilpatrick's Division. Farnsworth was killed. Merritt's Brigade of Buford's Division, which reached the field on the 3rd, engaged some of Longstreet's troops along the Emmitsburg Road. The accomplished object of these movements was to prevent Longstreet from giving assistance to the charge of Pickett on Meade's center.

THE CAVALRY FIGHT ON THE RIGHT FLANK.

As already noted, General Stuart in his movement in rear of the Army of the Potomac with three brigades of cavalry—Fitzhugh Lee's, Wade Hampton's, and Chambliss'—reached Hanover on June 30th, fought a battle in the streets, and moved on to Carlisle on the afternoon of July 1st. There he got in touch with the main Confederate Army, with which he had been out of communication for seven days.

After an encounter with a portion of Kilpatrick's forces at Hunterstown on the afternoon of July 2nd, he moved up to a position between the Hunterstown and Harrisburg roads on Ewell's left, expecting to reach Meade's rear about the time of Pickett's Charge on Meade's front. He was joined by Jenkins' Confederate Brigade of mounted infantry armed with Enfield rifles. Jenkins was wounded at Hunterstown, and the brigade and the command fell to Colonel Ferguson.

General Gregg, in command of the 2nd Cavalry Division of the Union Army, reached the field east of Gettysburg at the intersection of the Hanover and Low Dutch roads at 11 A. M. on July 2nd. In the afternoon he halted a movement of Walker's brigade of Johnson's Division, Ewell's Corps, in their movement from Brinkerhoff Ridge to assist in the attack on Meade's right at Culp's Hill. He bivouacked for the night near the bridge across White Run. On the morning of the 3rd he returned to the position of the 2nd, and took an active part in the cavalry fight on the right flank at the time of Pickett's Charge. In the afternoon, in the important engagement on East Cavalry Field he successfully opposed General Stuart in his efforts to get behind the Union line.

THE LOCATION.

East Cavalry Field is 3 miles east of Gettysburg and includes the territory lying between the York Pike on the north and the Hanover Road on the south. On the east it is bounded by the Low Dutch Road which intersects the Baltimore Pike at its southern end, and the York Pike at its northern end. Brinkerhoff Ridge, which crosses the Hanover Road at right angles about 1½ miles east of the town, forms its boundary on the west. Cress Ridge is formed by the elevation between Cress's Run on the west and Little's Run on the east. Both ridges right angle across the Hanover Road.

All the positions held by troops have been marked and the entire field is readily accessible over well-built roads and avenues. Because of its partial isolation from the principal fields, this important area is not visited as frequently as it should be.

GENERAL STUART'S PLAN.

General Stuart did not wish to bring on a general engagement. He expected his skirmishers to keep the Union Cavalry engaged while his other forces were moving undiscovered toward the rear of Meade's line. He says in his report:

"On the morning of July 3, pursuant to instructions from the commanding general, I moved forward to a position to the left of Gen. Ewell's left, and in advance of it, where a commanding ridge (Cress Ridge) completely controlled a wide plain of cultivated fields stretching toward Hanover, on the left, and reaching to the base of the mountain spurs, among which the enemy held position. My command was increased by the addition of Jenkins' Brigade, who here in the presence of the enemy allowed themselves to be supplied with but 10 rounds of ammunition, although armed with approved Enfield muskets.

"I moved this command and W. H. F. Lee's secretly through the woods to a position, and hoped to effect a surprise upon the enemy's rear, but Hampton's and Fitz Lee's Brigades, which had been ordered to follow me, unfortunately debouched into the open ground, disclosing the movement, and causing a corresponding movement of a large force of the enemy's cavalry."

It was the advance of Hampton and Fitzhugh Lee which caused Stuart's plans to miscarry.

Reaching East Cemetery Hill on the afternoon of the first day, General Hancock took command of the Union troops. On the second day the guns pointed downward to meet the onslaught of the Confederates

LITTLE ROUND TOP.—Its strategic importance was seen by General Warren who commanded it to be fortified and held

GENERAL GREGG'S REPORT.

On the Union side, General D. McM. Gregg had under his command three brigades of cavalry—one in command of General George A. Custer, who later was responsible for "Custer's Last Charge" in Indian warfare. General Gregg's report gives a brief description of the many charges and countercharges:

"A strong line of skirmishers displayed by the enemy was evidence that the enemy's cavalry had gained our right, and were about to attack, with the view of gaining the rear of our line of battle. The importance of successfully resisting an attack at this point, which, if succeeded in by the enemy, would have been productive of the most serious consequences, determined me to retain the brigade of the Third Division until the enemy were driven back. General Custer, commanding the brigade, fully satisfied of the intended attack, was well pleased to remain with his brigade. The First New Jersey Cavalry was posted as mounted skirmishers to the right and front in a wood. The Third Pennsylvania Cavalry deployed as dismounted skirmishers to the left and front in open fields, and the First Maryland on the Hanover turnpike, in position to protect the right of my line.

"The very superior force of dismounted skirmishers of the enemy advanced on our left and front required the line to be re-enforced by one of General Custer's regiments. At this time the skirmishing became very brisk on both sides, and the artillery fire was begun by the enemy and ourselves. During the skirmish of the dismounted men, the enemy brought upon the field a column for a charge. The charge of this column was met by the Seventh Michigan Cavalry, of the First (Second) Brigade, Third Division, but not successfully. The advantage gained in this charge was soon wrested from the enemy by the gallant charge of the First Michigan, of the same brigade. This regiment drove the enemy back

to his starting point, the enemy withdrew to his left, and on passing the wood in which the First New Jersey Cavalry was posted, that regiment gallantly and successfully charged the flank of his column. Heavy skirmishing was still maintained by the Third Pennsylvania Cavalry with the enemy, and was continued until nightfall. During the engagement, a portion of this regiment made a very handsome and successful charge upon one of the enemy's regiments. The enemy retired his column behind his artillery, and at dark withdrew from his former position. The fire of the artillery during this engagement was the most accurate that I have ever seen."

Stuart's forces numbered about 7,000, and Gregg and Custer's about 5,000.

LEE'S RETREAT.

On the night of the 3rd, Lee withdrew all his forces to Seminary and Snyder ridges. Orders were issued and instructions given for the retreat to the Potomac River at Williamsport and Falling Waters. The effectives moved to Fairfield over the Hagerstown or Fairfield Road. The wagon-train, 17 miles long, with the wounded, was moved by way of the Cashtown Road (Chambersburg Pike), under the command of Brigadier-General John D. Imboden, who has described his interview with General Lee at his headquarters, which were still located in an orchard in the rear of the Seminary buildings, as follows:

"He invited me into his tent, and as soon as we were seated he remarked: 'We must now return to Virginia. As many of our poor wounded as possible must be taken home. I have sent for you because your men and horses are fresh and in good condition, to guard and conduct our train back to Virginia. The duty will be arduous, responsible, and dangerous, for I am afraid you will be harassed by the enemy's cavalry. I can spare you as much artillery as you may require but no other troops, as I shall need all I have to return safely by a different and shorter route than yours. The batteries are generally short of ammunition, but you will probably meet a supply I have ordered from Winchester to Williamsport."

On account of a terrific rainstorm shortly after noon on the 4th there was considerable delay in getting the Confederate train started. Well guarded in front and rear, the head of the column near Cashtown was put in motion and began the ascent of the mountain. The wounded suffered indescribable hardships. Many had been without food for thirty-six hours, and had received no medical attention since the battle. Among the wounded officers were General Pender and General Scales. The trip cost Pender his life. General Imboden said:

"During this retreat I witnessed the most heartrending scenes of the War."

As a military movement the retreat was a success. Though harassed by pursuing forces, the train reached the Potomac with comparatively little loss.

The main Confederate Army crossed the mountain, principally at the Fairfield gap. On account of the heavy rain, Ewell's Corps, which brought up the rear did not leave Gettysburg until the forenoon of the 5th. Somewhat delayed, but not seriously impeded, Lee arrived at the Potomac on July 12, finding it too high to cross. There he entrenched his army. The next day, the waters having fallen, he got safely away.

No Pursuit by Meade.

Because of Lee's strong position, Meade made no countercharge. He had won a notable victory, and believed it unwise to risk undoing his work. His army had suffered heavily. Both armies moved south. The Confederate cause had received a severe blow. The defeat at Gettysburg and the surrender of Vicksburg on July 4th to Grant ended all hope of foreign recognition. Yet, for almost two years the desperate struggle was to continue!

The boulder-strewn face of Little Round Top, assaulted by brave
Confederates and held by brave Unionists

The Gettysburg Carnage.

The War records estimate the Union casualties, killed, wounded, and missing, at 23,000 of the 84,000 engaged. The Confederate casualties are estimated at over 20,000 of the 75,000 engaged. Approximately 10,000 bodies were left at Gettysburg for burial, and 21,000 living men to be healed of their wounds.

No words can picture the desolation of the little town. As the soldiers marched away, their places were taken by physicians and surgeons, nurses and orderlies, civilian as well as military, and the ministrations of mercy began. In these the citizens of Gettysburg, especially the women, took an important part. Hither came also a new army of parents and wives and brothers and sisters, seeking, sometimes with success, sometimes with grievous disappointment, for their beloved.

HAPPENINGS ON THE THIRD DAY

A Medal for Disobedience

On the afternoon of July 3rd, Captain William E. Miller, of Company H, 2nd Brigade, of Gregg's Division of Union Cavalry, made a charge against the Confederate Cavalry, in command of Major-General J. E. B. Stuart, in their movement from Cress Ridge, East Cavalry Field, to reach the rear of Meade's line at the time of Pickett's Charge.

The incident is described by Captain William Brooke Rawle, a participant in the charge, in his "History of the Third Pennsylvania Cavalry."

"When the cavalry fighting began, Captain Miller's squadron was stationed in Lott's woods to the west of the Low Dutch Road, beyond the Hanover Road, and was deployed, mounted as skirmishers, along the western edge of the woods. There was considerable long-range firing before the climax of the fighting came. About 3 o'clock in the afternoon . . . a large body of cavalry, which proved to be Hampton's and Fitzhugh Lee's brigades, was seen approaching in magnificent order, mounted, from the northern side of the field. Captain Miller and I rode out a few yards in front of our position to a slight rise in the ground to get a good view. The enemy quickened his pace, first to a trot, then to a gallop, and then the charge was sounded. The nearest available compact body of Union Cavalry at hand to meet the enemy was the 1st Michigan Cavalry of General Custer's brigade, which was serving temporarily under General Gregg. It was ordered to meet the enemy's charge by a counter-charge, although the Confederate brigade greatly outnumbered the Michigan regiment. Captain Miller and I saw at once that unless more men were sent against the enemy the Michigan regiment would be swept from the field. He said to me, 'I have been ordered to hold this position at all hazards, but if you will back me up if I get into trouble for exceeding my orders, I will make a charge with the squadron.' This was in order to make a diversion in favor of our troops, and help the Michigan men. I assured him in an emphatic manner that I would stand by him through thick and thin. He then ordered me to rally the left wing of the squadron while he did the same with the right. When this was done the squadron fired a volley into the Confederate column, which was within easy range. The men were very impatient to begin their charge, and the right wing, headed by Captain Miller, started off at a gallop.

"A stone and rail fence divided the line of the squadron front, running at right angles to it, and I had to make a slight detour to get around it with the left wing of the squadron. This, and the fact that the head of the squadron was headed to the right oblique, caused a gap of some thirty yards or so between the rear of the portion of the squadron under Captain Miller and myself with the left of the left portion. Meanwhile the two opposing columns had met, and the head of the Confederate column was fast becoming jammed, and the men on the flanks were beginning to turn back. Captain Miller, with his men struck the left flank of the enemy's column pretty well towards the rear, about two-thirds or three-fourths of the way down, and as the impetus of the latter had stopped while his men had full headway on, he drove well into the column and cut off its rear and forced it back in the direction whence it came, and the captain and some of his men got as far as the Rummel house. As to this last, I learned from the men engaged. Captain Miller was wounded in the arm during the fight.

"I myself with the rear portion of Captain Miller's squadron did not succeed in getting all the way through. Just as I and my men reached the flank of the enemy many of the latter were getting to the rear and we were swept along with the current and scattered, some of us, including myself, though narrowly escaping capture, succeeding in working our way in one's and two's to the right, where we got back into our lines again.

"The gallant conduct and dashing charge made by Captain Miller and his men were commented upon by all who saw it. A fact that made it all the more commendable was that it was done upon his own responsibility, without orders from a superior officer."

In July, 1897, a Congressional Medal of Honor was bestowed upon Captain Miller by direction of President McKinley, through the Secretary of War, General Russell A. Alger. The conferring of this tribute was especially appropriate, inasmuch as General Alger himself had participated on the right flank as the Colonel of the 5th Michigan, and was therefore eminently competent to decide.

The Wentz House

The Wentz house, which stands at the intersection of the Emmitsburg and Wheatfield roads, is now a Government-owned property, and is marked with an iron tablet with the inscription "Wentz House." It is not the house that was there at the time of the battle; the original building was dismantled and the present building erected on the same site.

At the time of the battle the house was owned and occupied by John Wentz, who cultivated the small tract of land belonging to it. He was twice married, and at this time was living with his second wife, who was the mother of Henry Wentz, the principal actor in an interesting incident of the battle of Gettysburg.

For many years before the beginning of the Civil War, carriage and coach-building was one of the leading industries of Gettysburg. Henry Wentz served an apprenticeship with the Ziegler firm of Gettysburg. He was frequently sent to deliver the products of the firm, and thereby became well acquainted with the different sections where sales were made.

In the early '50's he decided to move to Martinsburg, Va. (now W. Va.), and establish a carriage-building shop of his own. When a local military organization was formed and designated the "Martinsburg Blues," Henry became a member. Equipped with uniforms and arms, the members were drilled from time to time. Similar organizations were formed throughout the North as well as the South.

Most of the members of the Martinsburg Blues, including Henry Wentz, decided to cast their lot with the Southern cause, and were assigned to places in the armies of the South. But, by the irony of fate, he was destined to get back to his old home and command a battery posted back of the house on his father's land.

During the first day the Wentz property was not in danger, but when General Lee extended his line of battle south along the line of Seminary Ridge, and General Meade prolonged his line opposite on Cemetery Ridge in preparation for the battle of the second day, the Wentz family, with the exception of the father, decided to seek a safer location. On the night of the second day, after Sickles' advanced line at the Wentz house had been repulsed and occupied by the forces under General Lee, Henry Wentz visited his old home and was greatly surprised to find his father still there.

Early in the morning of the third day, 75 guns, in command of Colonel E. P. Alexander, were moved forward from Lee's first line to the line held by Sickles' advanced line on the second day. The battery in charge of Henry Wentz, who held the rank of lieutenant, was posted back of his old home, and he took an active part in the terrific artillery engagement prior to Pickett's Charge that ended on that part of the field. Henry's father kept to the cellar and, singularly, passed through it all unharmed and unhurt.

After the repulse of Pickett's Charge, the guns were withdrawn to their first line. During the night of the third day, Henry was anxious to know whether or not his father was still safe. He therefore went over to the house and found him fast asleep and unhurt in a corner of the cellar. Not wishing to disturb his much-needed rest, he found the stump of a candle, lit it, and wrote, "Good-bye and God bless you!" This message he pinned on the lapel of his father's coat and returned to his command preparatory to the retreat to Virginia.

Early on the morning of the 4th, the father awoke from his much-needed sleep and found that all the soldiers had departed. He then walked back to the ridge and saw Lee's army making hurried preparations for the retreat.

Fought with a Hatchet

At the battle of Gettysburg the 13th Vermont was a part of General Stannard's Vermont command. The 2nd Vermont brigade had been left on outpost duty in Virginia until the third day after the Army of the Potomac had passed in pursuit of Lee's troops into Maryland and Pennsylvania. Then the brigade got orders to proceed by forced marches to join the Army of the Potomac. The latter was also on a forced march, but in six days' time the Vermonters had overtaken the main body. Just before the first day's battle, Captain Brown's command came up to a well, at which was an armed guard. "You can't get water here," said the guard. " 'Gainst orders." "Damn your orders!" said Captain Brown, and then with all the canteens of the men, and with only one man to help him, he thrust the guard aside and filled the canteens. His arrest followed, and he was deprived of his sword.

When the battle began, Captain Brown was a prisoner. He begged for a chance to rejoin his company, and was allowed to go. His men were far away at the front, and he had no weapons. He picked up a camp hatchet and ran all the way to the firing-line, reached it, rushed into the fray, and singling out a Rebel officer 50 yards away, penetrated the Rebel ranks, collared the officer, wresting from him his sword and pistol, after which he dropped the hatchet, while his men cheered him amid the storm of bullets and smoke.

When the design for the 13th Vermont monument was made, it was the desire of the committee to have the statue represent Captain Brown, hatchet in hand. Accordingly, a model was prepared, but the Federal Government would not permit its erection. A second model was approved, showing Captain Brown holding a sabre and belt in his hand, the hatchet lying at his feet as though just dropped. The sabre depicted in the statue is an exact reproduction of the one captured.

This monument is on the east side of Hancock Avenue, near the large Stannard monument.

After the Battle

This is an extract from "Four Years with the Army of the Potomac," by Brigadier-General Regis de Trobriand, who commanded a brigade of Birney's Division of the 3rd Corps during the battle of Gettysburg:

"Between eight and nine o'clock in the evening of the 3rd, as the last glimmers of daylight disappeared behind us, I received an order to go down into the flat, and occupy the field of battle with two brigades in line. That of Colonel Madill was added to mine for that purpose. General Ward, who temporarily commanded the Division, remained in reserve with the 3rd.

"The most profound calm reigned now, where a few hours before so furious a tempest had raged. The moon, with her smiling face, mounted up in the starry heavens as at Chancellorsville. Her pale light shone equally upon the living and the dead, the little flowers blooming in the grass as well as upon the torn bodies lying in the pools of clotted blood. Dead bodies were everywhere. On no field of battle have I ever seen them in such numbers. The greater part of my line was strewn with them, and, when the arms were stacked and the men asleep, one was unable to say, in that mingling of living and dead, which would awake the next morning and which would not.

"Beyond the line of advanced sentinels, the wounded still lay where they had fallen, calling for assistance or asking for water. Their cries died away without any reply in the silence of the night, for the enemy was close by, and it was a dangerous undertaking to risk advancing into the space which separated us. In making an attempt, an officer of my staff drew three shots, which whistled unpleasantly near his ears. All labors of charity were necessarily put off till the next morning. It is sad to think that this was a sentence of death to numbers of the unfortunate. Mournful thoughts did not hinder the tired soldiers from sleeping. Everything was soon forgotten in a dreamless slumber.

"At dawn of day, when I awakened, the first object which struck my eyes was a young sergeant stretched out on his back, his head resting on a flat stone, serving for a pillow. His position was natural, even graceful. One knee slightly raised, his hands crossed on his breast, a smile on his lips, caused by a dream, perhaps, of her who awaited his return in the distant Green Mountains. He was dead. Wounded, he had sought out this spot in which to die. His haversack was near him. He had taken out of it a little book on which his last looks had been cast, for the book was still open in his stiffened fingers. It was the New Testament; on the first leaf a light hand had traced in pencil, some letters, rubbed out, which one might think were a name. I have kept the volume, and on the white space, to the unknown name I have added, 'Died at Gettysburg, July 3, 1863.'

"During the night, the enemy had drawn back his pickets to the other side of the Emmitsburg Road, and left us free access to assist the wounded. The appearance of litters and ambulance wagons strengthened them, by giving them hope. They related their engagements of the evening before, and their sufferings during the night. One of them, pointing out the dead lying around him, said: 'This one lived only till sundown; that one lasted until about midnight. There is one who was still groaning but an hour ago.'

"Continuing my walk, I came near a large isolated rock. It might have been eight or ten feet high, and fifteen or twenty feet broad. Rounding on the side towards the enemy, but flat as a wall on the opposite side, it had served as an advanced post for one of our companies, probably belonging to Stannard's brigade.

What had happened there? Had they been surprised by the rapid advance of the enemy? Had they tried to shelter themselves behind that stone during the fight? Had the firing of canister by our guns rendered retreat impossible? Had they refused to surrender? No one, to my knowledge, escaped to tell. Whatever was the cause, there were twenty lying there cut down by lead and steel, and amongst the pile I recognized the uniform of an officer and the chevrons of a sergeant.

"When I returned to the center of my line, the ambulances were at work, and squads detailed from each regiment picked up the arms which were scattered by thousands over the field. A little later my command was relieved, and again took its position of the evening before.

"Some reconnaissances sent out to look for the enemy had not far to go to find him. His pickets were still on the edge of the woods in front of the Seminary Heights. We afterwards learned that he expected, during the whole day, that we would attack, hoping to get revenge. But General Meade, content with his victory, would not take the risk of compromising it by leaving his position before Lee had abandoned his, in which he acted wisely, whatever may have been said to the contrary.

"The afternoon was thus spent in first picking up our wounded and afterwards those of the enemy. The ambulance wagons were hardly enough for the work. The litter-bearers placed the wounded along our lines, where they had to await their turn to be taken to the rear. We did what we could to make the delay as short as possible, for many of them were brave Southern boys, some having enlisted because they honestly believed it was their duty, others torn by force from their families, to be embodied in the Rebel army by the inexorable conscription. After the defeat, they were resigned, without boasting, and expressed but one wish: that the war would terminate as soon as possible, since the triumph of the North appeared to be but a question of time.

"I recall to mind a young man from Florida who told me his history. His name was Perkins, and he was scarcely twenty years old. The only son of aged parents, he had in vain endeavored to escape service. Tracked everywhere by the agents of the Richmond government, he had been forced to take up the musket, and had done his duty so well that he had been rapidly promoted to sergeant. In the last charge of the day before, he had had his left heel carried away by a piece of shell, and his right hand shattered by a canister shot. One amputation, at least, probably two, was what he had to expect; and yet he did not complain. But when he spoke of his aged parents awaiting his return, and of the sad condition in which he would re-enter the paternal home, his smile was more heart-breaking than any complaint. In order that his wounds might be sooner dressed, one of my aids, Lieutenant Houghton, let him have his horse, at the risk of marching on foot if we moved before he was returned.

"The next night we passed in the rain. It always rains on the day after a great battle. On the morning following we discovered the enemy to be in full retreat. Seeing that the attack he expected did not come off, and fearing for the safety of his communications with the Potomac, General Lee could do nothing else but retire through the mountains, which he did during the night of the 4th and 5th of July. Then only began that disorder in his columns, and that confusion, the picture of which has been somewhat exaggerated; an almost inevitable consequence, besides, to that kind of a movement. Our cavalry began to harass him on the flanks, while the 6th Corps, having remained intact, pressed on his rear-guard.

"The difficulties that General Sedgwick met in the Fairfield pass, where the enemy had intrenched, probably made General Meade fear that a direct pursuit would entail too great loss of time in the mountains. So, instead of following Lee in the valley of the Cumberland, he decided to march on a parallel line, to the east of the South Mountains."

THE BATTLE OF GETTYSBURG

An Honest Man

General E. P. Alexander, Chief of Artillery of Longstreet's Corps, tells of a trade that occurred during the retreat from Gettysburg:

"Near Hagerstown I had an experience with an old Dunkard which gave me a high and lasting respect for the people of that faith. My scouts had had a horse transaction with this old gentleman, and he came to see me about it. He made no complaint, but said it was his only horse, and as the scouts had told him we had some hoof-sore horses we should have to leave behind, he came to ask if I would trade him one of those for his horse, as without one his crop would be lost.

"I recognized the old man at once as a born gentleman in his delicate character-ization of the transaction as a trade. I was anxious to make the trade as square as circumstances would permit. So I assented to his taking a foot-sore horse, and offered him besides payment in Confederate money. This he respectfully declined. Considering how the recent battle had gone, I waived argument on the point of its value but tried another suggestion. I told him that we were in Maryland as the guests of the United States; that after our departure the Government would pay all bills left behind; and that I would give him an order on the United States for the value of his horse and have it approved by General Longstreet. To my surprise he declined this also. I supposed then that he was simply ignorant of the bonanza in a claim against the Government, and I explained that; and, telling him that money was no object to us under the circumstances, I offered to include the value of his whole farm. He again said he wanted nothing but the foot-sore horse. Still anxious that the war should not grind this poor old fellow in his poverty, I suggested that he take two or three foot-sore horses which we would have to leave anyhow, when we marched. Then he said, 'Well, sir, I am a Dunkard, and the rule of our church is an eye for an eye, and a tooth for a tooth, and a horse for a horse, and I can't break the rule.'

"I replied that the Lord, who made all horses, knew that a good horse was worth a dozen old battery scrubs; and after some time prevailed on him to take two, by calling one of them a gift. But that night we were awakened about midnight by approaching hoofs, and turned out expecting to receive some order. It was my old Dunkard leading one of his foot-sores. 'Well, sir,' he said, 'you made it look all right to me today when you were talking; but after I went to bed tonight I got to thinking it all over, and I don't think I can explain it to the church, and I would rather not try.' With that he tied old foot-sore to a fence and rode off abruptly. Even at this late day it is a relief to my conscience to tender to his sect this recogni-tion of their integrity and honesty, in lieu of the extra horse which I vainly en-deavored to throw into the trade. Their virtues should commend them to all financial institutions in search of incorruptible employees."

Extracts from the Diary of Colonel Fremantle

Colonel Fremantle, a member of the Cold Stream Guards, was a guest of the Army of Northern Virginia during the Gettysburg campaign. After the battle of Gettysburg, he returned to England and published "Three Months in the Southern States." The following is a vivid extract, describing a part of the battle from the Confederate lines.

"*July 1st (Wednesday)*. At 4.30 P.M. we came in sight of Gettysburg, and joined General Lee and General Hill, who were on the top of one of the ridges which form a peculiar feature of the country round Gettysburg. We could see the enemy retreating up one of the opposite ridges, pursued by the Confederates with loud yells. The position into which the enemy had been driven was evidently a strong one. His right appeared to rest on a cemetery, on the top of a high ridge to the right of Gettysburg, as we looked at it.

[56]

"General Hill now came up and told me he had been very unwell all day, and in fact he looks very delicate. He said he had two divisions engaged, and had driven the enemy four miles into the present position, capturing a great many prisoners, some cannon, and some colors. He said, however, that the Yankees had fought with a determination unusual to them.

"*July 2nd (Thursday).* At 2 P.M. General Longstreet advised me, if I wished to have a good view of the battle, to return to my tree of yesterday. I did so and remained there with Lawley and Captain Schreibert during the rest of the afternoon. But until 4.45 P.M. all was profoundly quiet, and we began to doubt whether a fight was coming off today at all. At that time, however, Longstreet suddenly commenced a heavy cannonade on the right. Ewell immediately took it up on the left. The enemy replied with equal fury, and in a few moments the firing along the whole line was as heavy as it is possible to conceive. A dense smoke arose for six miles; there was little wind to drive it away, and the air seemed full of shells— each of which appeared to have a different style of going, and made a different noise from the others. The ordnance on both sides is of a very varied description. Every now and then a caisson would blow up—if a Federal one, a Confederate yell would immediately follow. The Southern troops, when charging, or to express their delight, always yell in a manner peculiar to themselves. The Yankee cheer is much like ours, but the Confederate officers declare that the Rebel yell has a particular merit, and always produces a salutary effect upon their adversaries. A corps is sometimes spoken of as 'a good yelling regiment.'

"As soon as the firing began, General Lee joined Hill just below our tree, and he remained there nearly all the time, looking through his field-glasses, sometimes talking to Hill and sometimes to Colonel Long of his staff. But generally he sat quite alone on the stump of a tree. What I remarked especially was, that during the whole time the firing continued, he sent only one message, and received only one report. It evidently is his system to arrange the plan thoroughly with the three commanders, and then leave to them the duty of modifying and carrying it out to the best of their abilities.

"When the cannonade was at its height, a Confederate band of music, between the cemetery and ourselves, began to play polkas and waltzes, which sounded very curious, accompanied by the hissing and bursting of the shells.

"At 5.45 all became comparatively quiet on our left and in the cemetery; but volleys of musketry on the right told us that Longstreet's infantry were advancing, and the onward progress of the smoke showed that he was progressing favorably; but about 6.30 there seemed to be a check, and even a slight retrograde movement. . . . A little before dark the firing dropped off in every direction, and soon ceased altogether. We then received intelligence that Longstreet had carried everything before him for some time, capturing several batteries and driving the enemy from his positions; but when Hill's Florida brigade and some other troops gave way, he was forced to abandon a small portion of the ground he had won, together with all the captured guns, except three. His troops, however, bivouacked during the night on ground occupied by the enemy in the morning.

"*July 3rd (Friday).* At 2.30 P.M., after passing General Lee and his staff, I rode on through the woods in the direction in which I had left Longstreet. I soon began to meet many wounded men returning from the front; many of them asked in piteous tones the way to a doctor or an ambulance. The further I got, the greater became the number of the wounded. At last I came to a perfect stream of them flocking through the woods in numbers as great as the crowd in Oxford Street in the middle of the day. Some were walking alone on crutches composed of two rifles, others were supported by men less badly wounded than themselves, and others carried on stretchers by the ambulance corps, but in no case did I see a sound man helping the wounded to the rear unless he carried the red badge of the ambulance corps. They were still under heavy fire, the shells bringing down great limbs of trees, and carrying further destruction amongst this melancholy procession. I saw all this in much less time than it takes to write it, and although astonished to meet such vast numbers of wounded, I had not seen enough to give me any idea of the real extent of the mischief.

"When I got close up to General Longstreet, I saw one of his regiments advancing through the woods in good order; so, thinking I was just in time to see the attack, I remarked to the General that 'I wouldn't have missed this for anything.' Longstreet was seated at the top of a snake fence at the edge of the woods (Spangler Woods), and looking perfectly calm and imperturbed. He replied, laughing, 'The devil you wouldn't! I would like to have missed it very much; we've attacked and been repulsed: look there!'

"For the first time I then had a view of the open space between the two positions, and saw it covered with Confederates slowly and sulkily returning towards us in small broken parties, under a heavy fire of artillery. But the fire where we were was not so bad as further to the rear; for although the air seemed alive with shells, yet the greater number burst behind us. The General told me that Pickett's Division had succeeded in carrying the enemy's position and captured his guns, but after remaining there twenty minutes, it had been forced to retire on the retreat of Heth and Pettigrew on his left. . . . .

"Major Walton was the only officer with him (Longstreet) when I came up— all the rest had been put in the charge. In a few minutes Major Latrobe arrived on foot, carrying his saddle, having just had his horse killed. Colonel Sorrell was also in the same predicament, and Captain Goree's horse was wounded in the mouth. . . .

"Soon after I joined General Lee, who had in the meanwhile come to that part of the field on becoming aware of the disaster. If Longstreet's conduct was admirable, that of General Lee was perfectly sublime. He was engaged in rallying and in encouraging the broken troops, and was riding about a little in front of the woods, quite alone—the whole of his staff being engaged in a similar manner further to the rear. His face, which is always placid and cheerful, did not show signs of the slightest disappointment, or annoyance; and he was addressing to every soldier he met a few words of encouragement, such as, 'All this will come right in the end: we'll talk it over afterwards; but, in the meantime, all good men must rally. We want all good and true men just now.' He spoke to all the wounded men that passed him, and the slightly wounded he exhorted 'to bind up their hurts and take up a musket' in this emergency. Very few failed to answer his appeal, and I saw many badly wounded men take off their hats and cheer him. He said to me, 'This has been a sad day for us, Colonel—a sad day; but we can't expect always to gain victories.' He was also kind enough to advise me to get into some more sheltered position as the shells were bursting round us with considerable frequency. . . .

"I saw General Wilcox come up to him, and explain, almost crying, the state of his brigade. General Lee immediately shook hands with him and said cheerfully, 'Never mind, General, all this has been *my* fault—it is I that have lost this fight, and you must help me out of it in the best way you can.' In this manner I saw General Lee encourage and reanimate his somewhat dispirited troops, and magnanimously take upon his own shoulders the whole weight of the repulse."

GETTYSBURG AND ITS MILITARY PARK

THE Gettysburg National Military Park lies entirely within the limits of Adams County, Pennsylvania. Gettysburg, the county-seat, is situated about 8 miles from the Mason and Dixon's line, the southern boundary of the State. It was founded in 1780, and named for its founder, James Gettys.

At the time of the battle the town had a population of about 2,000. Little did the quiet inhabitants expect that its peaceful environs—Oak Hill, Seminary Ridge, Culp's Hill, Cemetery Hill, the Round Tops, and Devil's Den—would witness the most sanguinary struggle of the Civil War, and that Gettysburg would gain a lasting fame, unequaled by the most noted battlefields of the Old World. Not even the commanders, Meade and Lee, knew where they would meet in battle array. Like two giant stormclouds, the two armies neared each other for days, neither foreseeing where they would mingle their lightnings in the storm of battle. Advance forces met and clashed while making reconnaissances—and Gettysburg and its vicinity was selected by accident rather than by design.

What fame Gettysburg enjoyed was due chiefly to its College, then called Pennsylvania, now Gettysburg, and to its Lutheran Theological Seminary. The town had been the home for some years of Thaddeus Stevens, the "Great Commoner," life-long champion of human rights, savior of the free school system of Pennsylvania, and after his removal to Lancaster, in 1842, a brilliant leader in the House of Representatives during the war. The vicinity furnished its full quota of soldiers, though none of its companies except one, Company K, First Pennsylvania Reserves, participated in the battle, the rest being on duty elsewhere.

The population of Gettysburg has increased to 8000. The College and Seminary are still flourishing. The College has an enrollment of 2000 students. A Reserve Officers Training Corps has been added to the course, and students are being instructed in military tactics by United States Army officers.

The area of Gettysburg National Military Park, including East Cavalry Field 3 miles east of the town, and South Cavalry Field 3 miles south, is nearly 40 square miles. The part surrounding Gettysburg covers about 24 square miles, and was the scene of the principal engagements on July 1st, 2nd, and 3rd, 1863. The Government owns 4000 acres; the remainder is held by private owners.

The first organization in charge of the battlefield was the Gettysburg Battlefield Memorial Association, upon which the Legislature of Pennsylvania, on April 30th, 1864, conferred the rights of a corporation. In 1867–68 the Legislature appropriated $6,000 to be applied to the purchase of portions of the battle-grounds and the general purposes for which the Association was incorporated. The money was used to secure the portion of Culp's Hill upon which the breastworks were still standing; the section of East Cemetery Hill where Stewart's, Reynolds', Ricketts', Cooper's and Weidrick's batteries were posted, where the lunettes still remain; and also a small piece of ground on the slope and summit of Little Round Top. This purchase was the nucleus of what became, by additional purchases of the Association and later of the Gettysburg National Park Commission, the present Gettysburg National Military Park.

The Legislatures of the Northern States represented in the

VIEW FROM CULP'S HILL.—Gettysburg's fine trees. In the distance is the Phillipoteaux Cyclorama with its vivid representation of Pickett's Charge battle contributed various sums for the prosecution of the work, and from time to time new members of the Association were appointed. As the appropriations were received, additional land was acquired and avenues were laid out. The erection of monuments to the different regiments was begun by the State of Massachusetts in 1879. In 1894, the whole property, about 600 acres of land, with 17 miles of avenues, giving access to 320 monuments, was transferred to the United States Government. The Gettysburg National Military Park was established by Act of Congress, approved February 11th, 1895, and the Secretary of War appointed the Gettysburg National Park Commission: Colonel John P. Nicholson, Pennsylvania, Chairman, John B. Bachelder, Massachusetts, and Brigadier General William H. Forney, Alabama. Colonel E. B. Cope was selected as topographical engineer.

Upon the death of General Forney, Major William M. Robbins, of North Carolina, was appointed to fill the vacancy. John B. Bachelder was succeeded by Major Charles A. Richardson, of New York. On the death of Major Robbins, General L. L. Lomax, of Virginia, was appointed. General Lomax died May 28th, 1913, and Major Richardson on January 24th, 1917. Colonel Nicholson, the last surviving member of the Commission, died on March 8th, 1922. All Commissioners, with the exception of John B. Bachelder, served in the Battle of Gettysburg, and he reached the field immediately after the battle, continuing his interest and his historical researches until his death. On the death of Colonel Nicholson, Colonel E. B. Cope was appointed Superintendent.

The Park is a monument to the devotion of this Commission, in active operation for thirty years. Colonel Cope was succeeded (1931) by Colonel E. E. Davis, a native of Iowa, commissioned Major Quartermaster Reserve Corps, March 6th, 1917, who served overseas in the World War. Colonel Davis retired on July 16th, 1932. James R. McConaghie, native of Iowa, a graduate of Harvard College, 1st Lieutenant, 4th Infantry, 3rd Division in the World War, was appointed Superintendent February 8th, 1933.

The development begun by the Association included laying out of avenues and erecting of regimental monuments, but nothing was done toward converting the avenues into permanent roads. The different lines of battle were not accurately marked, and im-

JENNIE WADE HOUSE.—Here Jennie Wade was killed while baking bread. The house is practically unchanged; bullet-marks and other injuries have been preserved

portant sections of land remained in private hands. By the end of the year the new Commission had made preliminary survey of 20 miles of avenues and proposed avenues, and, the following year, began construction. Gradually the whole field was made accessible by almost 35 miles of telford and macadam avenues. These avenues show the important positions occupied by the contending forces. Stone bridges were built across the streams. Miles of pipe-fencing and post-and-rail fencing were constructed, the former along the avenues indicating the battle-lines and the latter to enclose the Government land. Five steel observation towers were erected on prominent points, affording views in all directions.

Three survive to this day and are open to the public. Only the towers on Big Round Top and The Ziegler's Grove area have been abandoned and removed. The tower at Robinson Avenue was partially dismantled, but it still affords an over-the-tree-top view of first day terrain. Three of the original concrete footings can still be seen at the summit of Big Round Top.

Markers also show the locations of the headquarters of the Commander-in-Chief, as well as of the corps commanders of both armies. Six equestrian statues have been erected by States; also, imposing

State monuments by New York, Pennsylvania, Virginia, North Carolina and Alabama. There are many smaller markers, placed by States and other organizations. Bronze statues of division and brigade commanders have been erected. There are a number of National Monuments; one in the National Cemetery, where Lincoln stood when making his immortal address at the dedication of the cemetery, November 19th, 1863; also one in the south end of the cemetery bearing a bust of Lincoln, and another on Hancock Avenue in memory of the troops of the Regular Army. All the positions held by the Regulars have been marked. The total number of monuments to date is 845. Four hundred and fifteen guns indicate the positions of the artillery brigades and battalions.

The relief maps of the Gettysburg National Military Park, on exhibition at the office in the Federal Building, in Gettysburg, were designed by the Engineer of the Commission, Colonel E. B. Cope, and built under his supervision. The largest reproduces 24 square miles and correctly delineates all the topographical features of the Park. Many of the monuments and markers erected by the Commission were also designed by Colonel Cope. The imposing stone gateway at the entrance to Hancock Avenue was proposed by the Chairman, Colonel Nicholson, and designed by the Engineer. This gateway is built of native granite taken from the battlefield.

Celebrations, reunions, dedications, and campfires almost without number have been held at Gettysburg, bringing to the field those who participated in the battle, their families and friends, and many other visitors. For many years, until a permanent camp was established at Mt. Gretna, the National Guard of Pennsylvania encamped on the field. The two greatest occasions were the Twenty-fifth Anniversary in 1888, and the Fiftieth Anniversary in 1913. The latter was attended by almost 55,000 survivors of the two armies. Ample accommodations were provided for their comfort and enjoyment. The time extended over a period of eight days, June 29th to July 6th, and every State in the Union was represented. The men who had met as mortal enemies fifty years before now met as brothers. The American soldier is not only a good fighter but also a good friend. Many donned their uniforms of '63, some of Blue and some of Gray, but in the wearers great changes had been wrought. The sturdy veterans who in the vigor of their youth met fifty years before in battle, returned grizzled with age and the ravages of war, many bearing scars. With keen interest, in pairs and groups, they moved from place to place relating to each other their experiences. In startling contrast to the 45,000 casualties of '63 there were only seven deaths,

and these from the infirmities of age and natural causes. The President of the United States and many able speakers from all sections of the country made addresses to large audiences. It was an event never to be forgotten and did much finally to heal the animosities engendered by the war.

On July 3, 1922, Marines from Quantico, Va., under the command of Brigadier-General Smedley D. Butler, repeated Pickett's Charge, and on July 4th conducted it as such a charge would be made with equipment and maneuvers of that era.

CULP'S HILL.—Here the Union troops held their line late in the afternoon of the second day.

President Harding, General Pershing, and many others prominent in the State and Nation enjoyed the display.

For many years the West Point Military Academy seniors visited the field, usually in the month of May, remaining several days in order to study the strategical and tactical features of the battle in preparation for a required thesis. These visits have been discontinued since World War I.

In May, 1917, a training-camp for World War soldiers was established within the limits of the Park. The 4th, 7th and 58th Regiments of U. S. Infantry were transferred from El Paso, Texas, augmented by recruits, and divided into six United States Regular Regiments, viz.: 4th, 7th, 58th, 59th, 60th, and 61st. After being trained they were sent either to other camps or to the battlefields of France. During the year 1918 a unit of Tank Service was trained on the battlefield.

The fortifications remaining within the park include a line of earthworks on Culp's Hill, which was thrown up by the Union troops of the 12th Corps. On East Cemetery Hill there are a number of lunettes at the position held by the Union batteries.

The stone wall along the west side of Hancock Avenue, extending from the Taneytown Road to some distance south of the Angle, where Armistead crossed it in Pickett's Charge, is well preserved, and practically the same as at the time of the battle. There are some stone walls on the south side of Little Round Top that were erected and used by the Union forces. At the base of Big Round Top and along Seminary Ridge are long stone walls, erected and used by the Confederates. The boulders in the vicinity of Devil's Den and the Round Tops afforded natural defences for both armies.

THE VIRGINIA MEMORIAL.—The bronze group represents the various arms of the Confederate service. Above is a portrait statue of General Lee. The Memorial is the work of F. W. Sievers.

A line of earthworks on South Hancock Avenue is still in good condition.

The physical features of the Park are both varied and interesting. Standing in bold relief in the background at a distance of about 8 miles is a continuation of the Blue Ridge, designated locally as the South Mountain. This range, bounding the Shenandoah Valley of Virginia and the Cumberland Valley of Pennsylvania, screened the advance of the Confederate Army, and it was at the Cashtown Gap that General Lee ordered a concentration of his forces before his advance on Gettysburg.

The entire surface of the Park consists of low ridges and intervening valleys, beginning on the north in Herr's Ridge, upon which Heth's Division was deployed at the opening of the battle on July 1st. Opposite this ridge, and extending in the same direction, is McPherson Ridge, where the Union cavalry forces under Buford were deployed. Along Willoughby Run, which flows between these ridges, the battle opened on July 1, 1863. The next elevation, immediately north and west of the town, is known as Oak Ridge at its northern extremity and as far south as the Chambersburg Pike; from this point to its southern extremity it is called Seminary Ridge, taking its name from the yet existing Lutheran Theological Seminary. It was held by the Union Army on the first day of the battle and formed its principal line of defence. On the second and third days it was the principal Confederate line.

Seminary Ridge at its southern extremity drops off to a small ravine beyond which is Warfield Ridge, which extends in a southerly direction opposite Big Round Top; this formed the right of the Confederate line of battle on the second and third days.

South and southwest of the town is Cemetery Ridge, of which Big Round Top and Little Round Top are spurs, named from the Evergreen Cemetery and the site of the National Cemetery after the battle.

Cemetery Ridge formed the main line of battle of the Union Army during the battles of the 2nd and 3rd. A short distance east of the cemetery it bends sharply to the right, forming two rocky and wooded prominences, Culp's Hill and Spangler's Hill. Between

RICKETTS' BATTERY.—Ricketts' Battery on East Cemetery Hill was remanned four times. Owing to the slope, the guns could not be sufficiently depressed, and the defenders fought with sticks and stones

GUNS SUPPORTING PICKETT'S CHARGE.—These guns took part in the great artillery duel which preceded Pickett's Charge

Seminary Ridge on the west and Cemetery Ridge on the east, a low ridge along the line of the Emmitsburg Road is designated Emmitsburg Road Ridge. This extends to the Peach Orchard. It was crossed on the afternoon of the 3rd by the assaulting column of Pickett's Charge, and is one of the interesting points of the battle. Another ridge on the west front of Little Round Top contains Devil's Den, a mass of enormous granite rocks, apparently tossed in confusion by some giant hand. In this picturesque spot Longstreet made his famous assault against the Union left on the afternoon of July 2nd. The trend of these various ridges conforms generally to that of the Blue Ridge.

There are no large streams on the battlefield. The largest is Marsh Creek, only a small part of which is within the Park area. On the east is Rock Creek, extending the whole length of the Park, so named on account of the immense boulders within the channel and along the borders. On the north and west of Gettysburg is Willoughby Run, also extending the entire length of the Park and flowing south to Marsh Creek. Another small stream is Plum Run, near the center, beginning on the Codori farm and running south through the gorge at the Round Tops; this was crossed and recrossed by both armies during the second and third days. Lying wholly within the Potomac basin, all the streams flow south.

The highest point within the Park is Big Round Top on the south, which rises to an elevation of 786 feet, and is visible for miles in all directions. From Big Round Top, Little Round Top, Culp's Hill, Cemetery Hill, and Oak Hill there are extensive panoramic views. Aside from the historic association there is much in the magnificent and beautiful scenery to interest the visitor. In the woods and meadows, in the glens and vales of the battlefield there are romantic and charming bits of landscape. The prospect from the National Cemetery as the sun disappears behind the South Mountain is one of great beauty and impressiveness.

A large portion of the Park is covered with timber, chiefly the different varieties of oak, hickory, ash, poplar, elm, gum, cedar, and pine. Many of the groves are forests primeval, and in the fall the lofty pines of Big Round Top, contrasting with the crimson of the gigantic oaks covering it from base to summit and the gray-lichened surface of the massive boulders, form a striking and beautiful picture. Much care is given to the protection of the groves, in order to preserve the original condition of the field. Tree-surgery has prolonged the lives of trees of special historic interest. Visitors return year after year in spring to see the glorious masses of dogwood and redbud.

CENTER OF UNION LINE.—The center of the Union line, showing the Angle and the rounded clump of trees toward which Pickett directed his charge

HIGH-WATER MARK.—This monument, erected close to the rounded clump of trees toward which Pickett directed his charge, marks the turning-point of the conflict

East Cavalry Field, 3 miles east of Gettysburg, is the point from which Stuart's Cavalry started to move round the right wing of the Union Army in order to reach the rear of Meade's line at the time of Pickett's Charge. South Cavalry Field, 3 miles south of Gettysburg, was held by Farnsworth's Brigade of Kilpatrick's Division, and Merritt's Brigade of Buford's Division. All these positions have been marked with suitable tablets. The Cavalry Fields, though not contiguous to the main field, are important parts of the National Military Park.

Gettysburg has two railroads: the Gettysburg, and the Western Maryland which is now part of the Chessie system. At one time, a spur of the Philadelphia and Reading RR wound through the battlefield to the base of Little Round Top. Laid primarily to bring monuments to the battlefield, an occasional excursion train brought railfans to the park. Roads radiate from the town like the spokes of a wheel, and these provide ample approaches. The Lincoln Highway (30), entering via the Chambersburg Pike and continuing on the York Pike, gives a through route from west to east, and the Harrisburg Road (15) leads directly to the State Capital. The Emmitsburg Road runs south-west to Emmitsburg, and thence to Frederick and Washington. The Baltimore Pike is a through route to Baltimore and the South. The Hanover Road runs to Hanover on the east. There are also the Taneytown and Hagerstown roads, the latter (present day Route 116) the line of General Lee's retreat.

THE SOLDIERS' NATIONAL CEMETERY

Of the eighty-three cemeteries in the United States dedicated exclusively to the burial of soldiers, that at Gettysburg was the first.

A few days after the battle, Governor A. G. Curtin, of Pennsylvania, solicitous for the welfare of the soldiers, came to Gettysburg and appointed David Wills, a leading attorney, to act as his agent in the work of establishing a cemetery. Correspondence with the governors of other States was begun. Grounds were selected by Mr. Wills, and by the direction of Governor Curtin purchased for the State of Pennsylvania, to provide a burial-place for soldiers who fell in the battle.

Lots in the cemetery were tendered without cost to each State having dead upon the field. The expense of removing the bodies, laying out, ornamenting and enclosing the grounds, erecting a lodge for the keeper, and erecting a suitable monument to the memory of the dead, was to be borne by the several States, assessed in proportion to their population.

The seventeen acres of land which were purchased lie on Cemetery Hill adjoining the Citizens' Cemetery, at the apex of what had been the triangular battle-line of the Union Army, and an important tactical position on July 2nd and 3rd. At the time of the battle this land was a cornfield, divided by stone fences which were used to great advantage by the infantry of the Union Army. The most elevated portions had been points of vantage for many batteries of artillery.

The land was surrounded on the west, east, and north by a substantial, well-built wall of native granite, topped by a heavy dressed coping. A division fence of iron was erected between the Soldiers' National Cemetery and the Citizens' Cemetery.

The plans and designs for the laying out of the cemetery were prepared by William Saunders, an able landscape gardener of the Department of Agriculture, Washington, D. C. A semi-circular plan for the arrangement of the graves was adopted. The ground allotted to each State converges upon a central point. The size of each plot was determined by the number of graves belonging to each State. The bodies were placed side by side in parallel trenches with a space of twelve feet to each parallel and with a grass path between the rows of graves. The outer section is lettered A, and so on in alphabetical order. Two feet of space was allowed to each body, and a person standing in the center of the semi-circle and facing the circumference reads the names from left to right. The bodies are laid with the heads towards the center. The headstones are uniform in size and contain the name, regiment and company of each soldier so far as it was possible to obtain them. Another lot was set apart for the soldiers of the Regular Army. The graves of the unknown dead are located at each end of the semi-circle.

On the 27th of October, 1863, the work of exhumation was begun under the supervision of Samuel Weaver, a citizen of Gettysburg. It was completed on March 18th, 1864. The number of bodies exhumed and interred in the cemetery was 3,512, including 158 taken up by the authorities of Boston. Of the total number, 979 were unknown. Later other bodies were discovered and added, and the total interred was 3,734. Many other Union dead were sent to their family burial places.

The Confederate bodies remained in the original trenches until 1870–73, when 3,320 were transferred to southern cemeteries.

The central point of the semicircle from which Lincoln delivered his address is now occupied by the National Monument, one of the finest on the field. It is 60 feet in height; the pedestal, 25 feet square at the base, is crowned by a colossal statue representing the Genius of Liberty. Projecting from the angles are four buttresses, each supporting an allegorical statue. War is personified by an American soldier. History, a figure with stylus and pen, records the achievements and names of the dead. Peace is typified by a statue of an American mechanic; Plenty by a female figure with a sheaf of wheat. The main die of the pedestal is panelled. Upon one of the panels is inscribed an extract from Lincoln's Address.

From the point where this monument stands, a magnificent view is presented to the beholder. Sloping gradually toward the north and the west, the entire cemetery is spread out as a beautiful panorama, showing on a carpet of green the semi-circle of graves, the driveways lined with rows of splendid maples, spruces, birches, magnolias, and many other trees, as well as many clumps of shrubbery filling the intervals between. A view from this point as the sun sinks behind the distant range of the South Mountain is one long to be remembered.

Standing at the upper end of the cemetery is a lesser monument in the form of an exedra, the center of which contains a bust of Lincoln. Two panels, one to the left, the other to the right, contain inscriptions; one giving David Wills' letter of invitation to President Lincoln to attend the dedicatory exercises on November 19th, 1863; the other, Lincoln's immortal address in its entirety.

Opposite this monument is the Rostrum from which the memorial addresses are now delivered. The first memorial exercise was held on May 30th, 1868, establishing a custom continued until this day. Among the speakers of recent years, either in the cemetery or on adjoining sections of the Park, have been Presidents Roosevelt, Taft, Wilson, Coolidge, and Hoover; Vice-President Curtis; Pennsylvania Governors Sproul and Pinchot, and Honorable James J. Davis.

AIRPLANE VIEW.—The National Cemetery with its curving rows of headstones

LINCOLN AT GETTYSBURG

No action of the battle itself has been more variously reported than the visit of President Lincoln at the time of the dedication of the National Cemetery on November 19, 1863. A wise collector and judge among many conflicting accounts is Dr. William E. Barton, noted Lincoln scholar, who in his "Lincoln at Gettysburg" has assembled all available material.

Dr. Barton gives various interesting reasons why Lincoln chose to come to Gettysburg, though his presence was not very earnestly desired by the committee of arrangements. His ability as anything but a political speaker had not been demonstrated, and it was feared that he might spoil the occasion. Until two weeks before the dedication, the only invitation sent him was one of the printed circulars mailed to all national officials, congressmen, and others.

He was eager, Dr. Barton thinks, to see the field of Gettysburg. He had rejoiced in the victory, and had deplored with equal earnestness Meade's cautious policy in making no pursuit. He wished to urge the people to renewed devotion to the cause which at that moment did not look altogether promising. He wished also, Dr. Barton believes, to counteract the impression made by a

NATIONAL MONUMENT.—On the site of National Monument stood the platform from which Abraham Lincoln delivered his immortal address

LINCOLN MEMORIAL.—Memorial in honor of Lincoln's Address
Henry K. Bush-Brown, Sculptor

cruel slander which had wide circulation. Again and again news-
papers inimical to him had published an account of his visit to the
Antietam battlefield a year earlier, asserting that he had asked
his friend Ward Hill Lamon to sing a ribald song as they drove
about among the unburied dead.

Lincoln turned a deaf ear to most slanders, but this touched
him to the quick. It was not unlikely that he longed to prove the
libel false by a visit to another battlefield. The story continued
to be told, however, throughout his life.

Following is Ward Hill Lamon's account of the visit to Gettysburg, from his "Recollections of Lincoln." It is the opinion of the
author of this book, an eye-witness, that the reception which
Lamon describes had other causes than failure to value Lincoln's
words. The address was intended to be merely a simple dedication
which would not naturally be followed by applause. The audience
had stood through the address of Edward Everett which occupied
two hours, and through a prayer and musical numbers in addition.
Many of the crowd were turning away—they turned back and
listened earnestly, but with no impulse to applaud.

At the time of the dedication, Mr. Lamon was chief marshal
of the parade and was with Lincoln on the platform when the
address was delivered. Lamon writes:

... A day or two before the dedication of the National Cemetery at Gettysburg,
Mr. Lincoln told me that he would be expected to make a speech on the occasion;

that he was extremely busy, and had no time for preparation; and that he greatly feared he would not be able to acquit himself with credit, much less to fill the measure of public expectation. From his hat (the usual receptacle for his private notes and memoranda) he drew a sheet of foolscap, one side of which was closely written with what he informed me was a memorandum of his intended address. This he read to me, first remarking that it was not at all satisfactory to him. It proved to be in substance, if not the exact words, what was afterwards printed as his famous Gettysburg speech.

After its delivery on the day of commemoration, he expressed deep regret that he had not prepared it with greater care. He said to me on the stand, immediately after concluding the speech: "Lamon, that speech won't scour! It is a flat failure, and the people are disappointed." (The word "scour" he often used in expressing his conviction that a thing lacked merit, or would not stand the test of close criticism or the wear of time.) He seemed deeply concerned about what the people might think of his address; more deeply, in fact, than I had ever seen him on any public occasion. His frank and regretful condemnation of his effort, and more especially his manner of expressing that regret, struck me as somewhat remarkable; and my own impression was deepened by the fact that the orator of the day, Mr. Everett, and Secretary Seward both coincided with Mr. Lincoln in his unfavorable view of its merits.

The occasion was solemn, impressive, and grandly historic. The people, it is true, stood apparently spellbound; and the vast throng was hushed and awed into profound silence while Mr. Lincoln delivered his brief speech. But it seemed to him that this silence and attention to his words arose more from the solemnity of the ceremonies and the awful scenes which gave rise to them, than anything he had said. He believed that the speech was a failure. He thought so at the time, and he never referred to it afterwards, in conversation with me, without some

The Rostrum.—From the vine-draped Rostrum many famous speakers have addressed the throngs that visit Gettysburg on Memorial Day

expression of unqualified regret that he had not made the speech better in every way.

On the platform from which Mr. Lincoln delivered his address, and only a moment after it was concluded, Mr. Seward turned to Mr. Everett and asked him what he thought of the President's speech. Mr. Everett replied, "It is not what I expected from him. I am disappointed." Then in his turn Mr. Everett asked, "What do you think of it, Mr. Seward?" The response was, "He has made a failure, and I am sorry for it. His speech is not equal to him." Mr. Seward then turned to me and asked, "Mr. Marshal, what do you think of it?" I answered, "I am sorry to say that it does not impress me as one of his great speeches."

In the face of these facts it has been repeatedly published that this speech was received by the audience with loud demonstrations of approval; that "amid the tears, sobs, and cheers it produced in the excited throng, the orator of the day, Mr. Everett, turned to Lincoln, grasped his hand and exclaimed, 'I congratulate you on your success!' adding in a transport of heated enthusiasm, 'Ah, Mr. President, how gladly would I give my hundred pages to be the author of your twenty lines!'" Nothing of the kind occurred. It is a slander on Mr. Everett, an injustice to Mr. Lincoln, and a falsification of history. Mr. Everett would not have used the words attributed to him, in the face of his own condemnation of the speech uttered a moment before, without subjecting himself to the charge of being a toady and a hypocrite; and he was neither one or the other.

As a matter of fact, the silence during the delivery of the speech, and the lack of hearty demonstrations of approval immediately after its close, were taken by Mr. Lincoln as certain proof that it was not well received. In that opinion we all shared. If any person then present saw, or thought he saw, the marvelous beauties of that wonderful speech, as intelligent men in all lands now see and acknowledge them, his superabundant caution closed his lips and stayed his pen. Mr. Lincoln said to me after our return to Washington, "I tell you, Hill, that speech fell on the audience like a wet blanket. I am distressed about it. I ought to have prepared it with more care." Such continued to be his opinion of that most wonderful of all his platform addresses up to the time of his death.

HARVEST

Only the seasons and the years invade
   These quiet wheatfields where the Armies crashed,
And mockingbirds and quail fly unafraid
   Within the forest where the rifles flashed.
Here where the bladed wings of death have mown
   And gleaned their harvestry of golden lives,
The fruitful seeds of corn and wheat are sown,
   And where the cannon smoked, an orchard thrives.

Long are the war years over, with their pain,
   Their passionate tears and fury, and the sun
Lies hot and yellow on the heavy grain,
   And all the fighting on these fields is done.
But in their peace, the quivering heart recalls
   The youth that bled beside these old stone walls.

—AGNES KENDRICK GRAY.

By Permission of the Author.

BIBLIOGRAPHY

The principal source of data for this work is the "War of the Rebellion Official Records of the Union and Confederate Armies." The appended list of other sources has been made for those who wish to make an extended study.

Annals of the War . . . . McClure
Attack and Defense of Little Round Top . . . . Norton
Abraham Lincoln . . . . Charnwood
Abraham Lincoln, Life of . . . . Barton
Battles and Leaders, 4 vols. . . . . Century Co.
Battle of Gettysburg . . . . Young
Battle of Gettysburg . . . . Comte de Paris
Battle of Gettysburg . . . . Haskell
Barlow, Major-General, at Gettysburg . . . . N. Y. Mon. Com.
Campaign and Battle of Gettysburg . . . . Fiebeger
Campaigns of the Civil War . . . . Geer
Civil War Papers . . . . Mass. O. L. L.
Chancellorsville and Gettysburg . . . . Doubleday
Confederate Portraits . . . . Bradford
Four Years with the Army of the Potomac . . . . . . de Trobriand
From Manassas to Appomattox . . . . Longstreet
Gettysburg Then and Now . . . . Vanderslice
Gregg's Cavalry Fight at Gettysburg . . . . Rawle
Hays, Gen. Alexander, Life and Letters . . . . Fleming
Lee, Gen. R. E., Recollections and Letters of . . . . . Capt. R. E. Lee
Lee, Gen. R. E., Personal Reminiscences of . . . . . . Jones
Lee, Gen. R. E., Memoirs of . . . . Long
Lincoln and His Generals . . . . Macartney
Maine at Gettysburg . . . . Maine Com.
Meade, Maj.-Gen., Life of . . . . Bache
Meade at Gettysburg, With . . . . George G. Meade
Meade, General George Gordon . . . . Pennypacker
Military Memoirs of a Confederate . . . . Alexander
Numbers and Losses in the Civil War . . . . Livermore
New York at Gettysburg, 3 vols. . . . . N. Y. Mon. Com.
Pennsylvania at Gettysburg . . . . Pa. Mon. Com.
Recollections of Lincoln . . . . Lamon
Regimental Losses in the Civil War . . . . Fox
The War between the States . . . . Stevens
The War between the Union and the Confederacy . . . . Oates
Reminiscences of the Civil War . . . . Gordon
Stuart's Cavalry in the Gettysburg Campaign . . . . . . Mosby

In addition to the many histories and biographies which include the battle among their subjects, there are novels, short stories, and poems whose authors have made a careful study of Gettysburg as a background. Among them are the following:

John Brown's Body—Benet
Cease Firing—Johnston
Gettysburg: Stories of the Red Harvest and the Aftermath—Singmaster

For Young People
Emmeline—Singmaster
A Boy at Gettysburg—Singmaster
Sewing Susie—Singmaster

ORGANIZATION OF THE ARMY
OF THE POTOMAC
Major-General George G. Meade

First Corps
John F. Reynolds, Major General
John Newton, Major General

Divisions	Brigades
1. James S. Wadsworth Brigadier General	1. Solomon Meredith, Brig. Gen. 2. Lysander Cutler, Brig. Gen.
2. John C. Robinson Brigadier General	1. Gabriel R. Paul, Brig. Gen. 2. Henry Baxter, Brig. Gen.
3. Abner Doubleday Major General	1. Thomas Rowley, Brig. Gen. 2. Roy Stone, Col. 3. George J. Stannard, Brig. Gen.

Second Corps
Winfield S. Hancock, Major General

Divisions	Brigades
1. John C. Caldwell Brigadier General	1. Edward E. Cross, Col. 2. Patrick Kelly, Col. 3. Samuel K. Zook, Brig. Gen. 4. John R. Brooke, Col.
2. John Gibbon Brigadier General	1. William Harrow, Brig. Gen. 2. Alexander Webb, Brig. Gen. 3. Norman J. Hall, Col.
3. Alexander Hays Brigadier General	1. Samuel S. Carroll, Col. 2. Thomas A. Smyth, Col. 3. George L. Willard, Col.

Third Corps
Daniel E. Sickles, Major General

Divisions	Brigades
1. David D. Birney Major General	1. Charles K. Graham, Brig. Gen. 2. J. H. Hobart Ward, Brig. Gen. 3. Regis de Trobriand, Col.
2. Andrew A. Humphreys Brigadier General	1. Joseph B. Carr, Brig. Gen. 2. Wm. R. Brewster, Col. 3. George C. Burling. Col.

ORGANIZATION OF THE ARMY OF THE POTOMAC, continue

Fifth Corps
George Sykes, Major General

Divisions	Brigades
1. James Barnes Brigadier General	1. William S. Tilton, Col. 2. Jacob B. Sweitzer, Col. 3. Strong Vincent, Col.
2. George Sykes Major General Romeyne B. Ayres Brigadier General	1. Hannibal Day, Col. 2. Sidney Burbank, Col. 3. Stephen Weed, Brig. Gen.
3. Samuel W. Crawford Brigadier General	1. William McCandless, Col. 2. Joseph W. Fisher, Col.

Sixth Corps
John Sedgwick, Major General

Divisions	Brigades
1. Horatio G. Wright Brigadier General	1. Alfred T. A. Torbet, Brig. Gen. 2. Joseph J. Bartlett, Brig. Gen. 3. David A. Russell, Brig. Gen.
2. Albion P. Howe Brigadier General	1. Lewis A. Grant, Col. 2. Thomas H. Neill, Brig. Gen.
3. John Newton Major General Frank Wheaton Brigadier General	1. Alexander Shaler, Brig. Gen. 2. Henry L. Eustis, Col. 3. Frank Wheaton, Brig. Gen.

Eleventh Corps
Oliver O. Howard, Major General

Divisions	Brigades
1. Francis C. Barlow Brigadier General	1. Leopold von Gilsa, Col. 2. Adelbert Ames, Brig. Gen.
2. Adolph von Steinwehr Brigadier General	1. Charles Coster, Col. 2. Orlando Smith, Col.
3. Carl Schurz Major General	1. Alexander Schimmelfennig, Brig 2. W. Krzyzanowski, Col.

ORGANIZATION OF THE ARMY OF THE POTOMAC, continued

Twelfth Corps
Henry W. Slocum, Major General

Divisions	Brigades
1. Alpheus S. Williams Brigadier General	1. Archibald L. McDougal, Col. 2. Henry H. Lockwood, Brig. Gen. 3. Thomas H. Huger, Brig. Gen.
2. John W. Geary Brigadier General	1. Charles Candy, Col. 2. George A. Cobham, Col. 3. George S. Greene, Brig. Gen.

Cavalry
Alfred Pleasanton, Major General

Divisions	Brigades
1. John Buford Brigadier General	1. William Gamble, Col. 2. Thomas C. Devin, Col. 3. Wesley Merritt, Brig. Gen.
2. David McM. Gregg Brigadier General	1. John B. McIntosh, Col. 2. Pennock Ruey, Col. 3. J. Irvin Gregg, Col.
3. Judson Kilpatrick Brigadier General	1. Elon J. Farnsworth, Brig. Gen. 2. George A. Custer, Brig. Gen.

Chief of Artillery, Brigadier-General Henry J. Hunt
Number of guns belonging to the Artillery, 362
Number of guns at Gettysburg, 354

ORGANIZATION OF THE ARMY OF NORTHERN VIRGINIA
General Robert E. Lee

First Corps
James E. Longstreet, Lieutenant General

Divisions	Brigades
1. Lafayette McLaws Major General	1. John B. Kershaw, Brig. Gen. 2. William Barksdale, Brig. Gen. 3. Paul J. Semmes, Brig. Gen. 4. William T. Wofford, Brig. Gen.
2. George E. Pickett Major General	1. Richard B. Garnett, Brig. Gen. 2. James L. Kemper, Brig. Gen. 3. Lewis A. Armistead, Brig. Gen.
3. John B. Hood Major General	1. Evander Law, Brig. Gen. 2. Jerome B. Robertson, Brig. Gen. 3. George T. Anderson, Brig. Gen. 4. Henry L. Benning, Brig. Gen.

[79]

ORGANIZATION OF THE ARMY OF NORTHERN VIRGINIA, continued

Second Corps
Richard S. Ewell, Lieutenant General

Divisions	Brigades
1. Jubal A. Early Major General	1. Harry T. Hays, Brig. Gen. 2. Robert F. Hoke (Isaac E. Avery), Brig. Gen. 3. William Smith, Brig. Gen. 4. John B. Gordon, Brig. Gen.
2. Edward Johnson Major General	1. George H. Steuart, Brig. Gen. 2. James A. Walker, Brig. Gen. 3. Francis T. Nicholls (J. M. Williams) Brig. Gen. 4. John M. Jones, Brig. Gen.
3. Robert E. Rodes Major General	1. Junius Daniel, Brig. Gen. 2. Alfred Iverson, Brig. Gen. 3. George Doles, Brig. Gen. 4. Stephen D. Ramseur, Brig. Gen. 5. Edward A. O'Neil, Brig. Gen.

Third Corps
Ambrose P. Hill, Lieutenant General

Divisions	Brigades
1. Richard H. Anderson Major General	1. Cadmus M. Wilcox, Brig. Gen. 2. Ambrose R. Wright, Brig. Gen. 3. William Mahone, Brig. Gen. 4. Edward A. Perry (David Lang), Brig. Gen. 5. Garnet Posey, Brig. Gen.
2. Henry Heth Major General	1. James J. Pettigrew, Brig. Gen. 2. John M. Brockenbrough, Col. 3. James J. Archer, Brig. Gen. 4. Joseph R. Davis, Brig. Gen.
3. William D. Pender Major General	1. James H. Lane, Brig. Gen. 2. Edward L. Thomas, Brig. Gen. 3. Alfred M. Scales, Brig. Gen. 4. Samuel McGowan (Abner Perrin), Brig. Gen.
4. James E. B. Stuart Major General (Cavalry)	1. Wade Hampton, Brig. Gen. 2. Beverly H. Robertson, Brig. Gen. 3. Fitzhugh Lee, Brig. Gen. 4. Wm. H. F. Lee (John R. Chambliss) Brig. Gen. 5. William E. Jones, Brig. Gen.
Valley District and Department of Western Virginia (Cavalry and mounted Infantry).	1. Albert G. Jenkins, Brig. Gen. 2. John D. Imboden, Brig. Gen.

Chief of Artillery, William N. Pendleton
Number of guns, 272

Index

Reproduction Of Title Page of First
"The Battle of Gettysburg"

A 1931 edition cover.

This the only known copy of the first ed-
tion of *The Battle of Gettysburg*. It was fou
among the effects of Nina Storrick, the auth
daughter (see Dedication, page 2), in the su
mer of 1980. It is a signed copy given to
author's sister in 1931. An inscription rea
"To: Anna S. Brinkirhoff. With best wishes
your brother Will."

This newest version is essentially equal
the first edition. All the original photogra
have been retained. The few textual chan
typically update physical status (such as the
duction of the five original steel observat
towers to three, the population of Gettysburg, etc.). All upda
material is printed in slightly larger type.

We trust this book will help you gain both insight and understa
ing to the causes, conditions and results of events that took place h
in 1863.

THE BATTLE
OF GETTYSBURG

The Country
The Contestants
The Results

BY

W. C. STORRICK

Retired Superintendent of Guides. For Twenty Years Connected with the
Gettysburg National Park Commission